To
Christi...

Vue Berry

♡

Happy Reading !
Happy Cooking !
Connie H Herbert

ROOTS and RECIPES

Down Through the Ages. Vern Berry holds her family cookbook.
Photo taken by Connie Heckert.

ROOTS and RECIPES

Six Generations of Heartland Cookery

Vern Berry with Connie Heckert

PELICAN PUBLISHING COMPANY
Gretna 1995

The word "Pelican" and the depiction of a pelican are trademarks
of Pelican Publishing Company, Inc.,
and are registered in the U.S. Patent and Trademark Office.

Library of Congress Cataloging-in-Publication Data

Berry, Vern, 1906-
    Roots and recipes : six generations of heartland cookery / by Vern
Berry with Connie Heckert.
        p.   cm.
    Includes bibliographical references and indexes.
    ISBN 1-56554-041-7
    1. Cookery, American. 2. Frontier and pioneer life—Middle West-
-History. I. Heckert, Connie K. II. Title.
TX715.B48533 1995
641.5973—dc20   93-44949
                                                                      CIP

Manufactured in the United States of America

Published by Pelican Publishing Company, Inc.
1101 Monroe Street, Gretna, Louisiana 70053

To my daughters, Barbara Berry Laake
and Doris Berry Meier

V.B.

To my mother-in-law,
Genevieve Ruth Lundberg Heckert (1911-1989)
and my mother,
Lavone Jane Morlan Delp (1916-1991)

C.H.

Contents

Grandma's Cookbook

I found a yellowed cookbook
One dreary rainy day
As I searched among old treasures
That Grandma'd packed away.

Do you know your grandma's cookbook
Is like a history of the ages?
I remembered all my childhood days
As I turned its yellowed pages.

Chicken bubbling in a pot,
Homemade noodles laid to dry.
A cup of this, a pinch of that,
That's what the old book says.

Marching through my memory
Come joys of long-gone days.

Acknowledgments

Many people need to be acknowledged for their contributions to the final manuscript of this cookbook project. I want to thank each of the pioneer women in this book, for they are my heritage: Elizabeth, Sarah, Elizabeth Jane, Lavina, and my mother, Jessie. I have gleaned something special from each of them. I want to thank my daughters, Barbara and Doris, and my sisters, Irene and Jerry, for encouraging me to attempt this project in my elder years. Their support has never wavered.

Research is an important part of such a book as this. Even though recipes have been handed down in my family, they were, for the most part, not written well or completely, and needed to be researched and supplemented for modern-day cooks. Collections from midwestern universities' archives were utilized when necessary: Augustana College, Rock Island; the University of Western Illinois, Macomb; and the University of Iowa, Iowa City. Judy Belan, rare books librarian at Augustana College and Marla Vizdal, archives specialist at the University of Western Illinois were very helpful. Robert McCown, head of special collections and manuscripts, and David Schoonover, curator of rare books, were invaluable with their assistance at the University of Iowa libraries.

Special thanks go to Chef Louis Szathmary II of Chicago, who donated a number of rare cooking recipes and books to the University of Iowa collection—more than twenty thousand separate items in classical and modern languages covering comprehensive culinary subjects, languages, time periods, and forms of publications. Helen Burkhiser, an Illinois-based expert on Laura Ingalls Wilder, pioneer cookery and life, offered her advice and expertise. Countless friends and acquaintances offered generous support simply by inquiring about the cookbook's progress.

In December 1990, when faced with the hurdle of testing recipes,

9

Wynne Schafer and Bonnie Moeller, both of Bettendorf, responded with enthusiasm, support, and suggestions of names of experienced testers who might help us. Wynne and Bonnie, at that point, kept the cookbook project alive. To each of our testers, we offer heartfelt gratitude: Ann Abplanalp; Karen Anderson and the department of home economists at Moline High School—Lori Clancy, Karon McAvoy, and Becky Sample; Debbie Bohman; Melisa Breheny; Roma Brown; Annabel DeCock; Bonnie Fox; Fern Hahn; Jan Harper; Deb Holmes; Deb Huebner; Cathy Johnson; Jeanette Keppy; Jan McCabe; Nancy Oppenheimer; Jan Pulley; Cindee Schnekloth; Cathy Spitzfaden; and Mary Kae Waytenick. Connie's sister, Karol Freund, helped with first and second testings.

Our Pen Women friends—members of the Quad-Cities branch of the National League of American Pen Women, Inc.—offered tremendous support and encouragement during this long project. Sidney Jeanne Seward, Chris Walkowicz, Delores Kuenning, Judie Gulley, and Pat Welch read parts of the manuscript and offered suggestions. After the original cookbook manuscript was stolen during a vacation, it was Evelyn Witter who kept urging me to start over.

When Iowa State University Press home economists suggested a reorganization of the format for this cookbook, it was John Heckert who helped with his computer expertise. To all of these people, we offer our gratitude.

Many many thanks to Dr. Calhoun, Nina Kooij, and Carolyn Ferrari at Pelican Publishing Company for their time and support for this project.

Finally, there is one person whose support and expertise bolstered our courage to push on toward our goal and bring closure to this project: Elizabeth "Liz" Meegan, food editor for *The Dispatch,* Moline, Illinois; *The Rock Island Argus,* Rock Island, Illinois; and *The Leader,* Scott County, Iowa.

Introduction

A librarian at the Department of Research and Record in Colonial Williamsburg, Genevieve Yost, has written that the first cookbook was published in the American colonies in 1742. It was *The Compleat Housewife or Accomplish'd Gentlewoman's Companion* by E. Smith. Later, it was reprinted in a fifth edition with an English title.

Fifty-four years later, Yost reported, an American was first credited with compiling a cookbook called *American Cookery* by Amelia Simmons, which was printed by Hudson and Goodwin of Hartford, Connecticut. However, it was William Parks, of Williamsburg, Virginia, who printed *The Compleat Housewife* and is credited with inaugurating the American publication of cookbooks.

Early American cookbooks, particularly in the Midwest, often are difficult to locate. Yost explained in a 1938 edition of *William and Mary Quarterly* why she felt there was a scarcity of records of cookbooks:

> These manuals were considered a working tool of the kitchen rather than an accession of the library. Perhaps they received such hard usage and were so worn and damaged that, having no intrinsic literary value, they were seldom preserved. . . . That recipes were handed down in manuscript volumes from one generation to another as prized family possessions is well known, and the early housewife may have relied on these manuscript collections and on memory.

The situation didn't change that much by the early 1900s. In their preface to *The New Household Discoveries*, written by Sidney Morse and published five times beginning in 1908, the publishers suggested, "Nearly every woman, when she marries and begins housekeeping, copies into a scrapbook the favorite recipes that have been handed down in her immediate family from mother to daughter for generations."

11

The Pioneers
in Vern Berry's Story

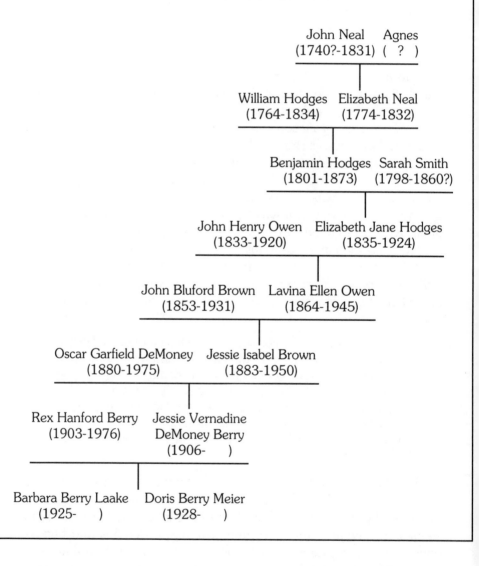

John Neal   Agnes
(1740?-1831)   (?   )
_____

William Hodges   Elizabeth Neal
(1764-1834)   (1774-1832)
_____

Benjamin Hodges Sarah Smith
(1801-1873)   (1798-1860?)
_____

John Henry Owen   Elizabeth Jane Hodges
(1833-1920)   (1835-1924)
_____

John Bluford Brown   Lavina Ellen Owen
(1853-1931)   (1864-1945)
_____

Oscar Garfield DeMoney   Jessie Isabel Brown
(1880-1975)   (1883-1950)
_____

Rex Hanford Berry   Jessie Vernadine
(1903-1976)   DeMoney Berry
                    (1906-   )
_____

Barbara Berry Laake   Doris Berry Meier
(1925-   )   (1928-   )

Laura Ingalls Wilder, through her books on pioneer childhood published in the 1930s and 1940s, has contributed greatly to the history of documented pioneer recipes. For the most part, however, early family favorites were passed down from generation to generation, or to a neighbor "over the backyard fence."

Cooking was more simple then because ingredients were basic. At the same time, it was more difficult because of the quantities necessary to feed large families and the lack of cooking technology. Always, the Berry family "made do" with what we could afford to buy or what we had in the cupboard or in the garden.

I cherish my family's cooking heritage and the women who came before me. It is so important to me that I have willed one of my most treasured possessions, an 1889 family cookbook, *The Everyday Cookbook: An Encyclopedia of Practical Recipes* to my granddaughter.

Perhaps I am a bit sentimental, but I had no idea how my life would be changed by a gift from my niece, Janet Pease. As I opened the brightly wrapped package, I found something inside that meant a lot to a woman in her eighty-second year. It was a family genealogy. Reading it, I was fascinated by the travels of my ancestors and the hardships of the pioneer women. Reflecting on the times in which they lived and comparing them with my own life, I began to see tremendous changes in kitchens, food preparations, and even the way recipes were recorded.

Regrettably, I have no pictures of my earliest ancestors. Knowledge of our early family history is based on a meticulously researched genealogy chart. It tells me that William Hodges and Elizabeth Neal were married in Henderson County in Kentucky in November of 1797. They had crossed the Cumberland Gap with their families. From other readings, I've discovered that this pioneer couple would have worked very hard to prepare for and live their life together. Neighbors and friends would have helped Will raise a cabin. Elizabeth and her family would have spun and woven wool for their clothes. Working together, the women would have gathered herbs for medicines and stored foods in a cave for winter.

Hardworking pioneer housewives, such as my ancestors, used whatever was available to them to survive. I call them "unsung heroines" in the history of this country. It was out of respect and admiration for these women that I began to trace my ancestors down through the centuries, as they used fireplace cooking—the simple preparation of meals in a spider, or iron pot hung in the fireplace—and progressed to cook stoves, kerosene stoves, and today's modern ranges.

As the methods of cooking changed, so did the recipes. The earliest recipes in this book, found at the beginning of each chapter of recipes, were originally simplistic. The women didn't measure ingredients as we would today. There were no oven temperatures or pan sizes to worry about. Few women could read or write, and they didn't record directions for their family favorites. Life was more basic then, and it wasn't difficult to remember ingredients or steps for preparation. As time passed, recipes became more explicit and detailed.

My own recipes have been handed down from generation to generation, and I have added recipes to my collection from friends and neighbors at social gatherings or "over the backyard fence." For more than fifty years, I cooked for my family, entertained at card clubs and church circles, made dinners for company, and planned party brunches. Like my pioneer ancestors, I "made do" when ingredients were unavailable or guests were unexpected—during the dust storms and depression years, for example. Later on, I moved on to better times and better living.

All of my life, I've found a strong sense of satisfaction in using foods and entertaining with my finest linens and dishes—even if they weren't so fine by someone else's standards. More important, I treasure the memories I have of good times with family and friends. To me, there is a quality of life that has been nourished in the heartland, and although it seems to be changing, it still retains its finest qualities of home and family.

Today, not many women entertain with big Sunday dinners as our grandmothers did. Appliances and preparations of foods continue to advance, leaving many traditions and favorite family recipes filed away with the spatters of cake batter dried and fading on them.

Today, packaged and frozen foods and the microwave oven have shortened our hours in the kitchen. Will our next generations think it strange that anyone ever baked cookies or rolled out a pie crust at home? Hopefully not. This concern is one of my most important reasons for pursuing publication of this cookbook—so my cherished recipes can not only be shared, but they will be recorded for those modern pioneer women with a love for homemade cookery who follow me.

The Generations

"Why not come along?" Dad urged. "You'll find work out there!"

My parents, Jessie and Oscar DeMoney, were moving the family from Iowa to "healthy" Colorado. It didn't take much persuasion. Life was easy in 1927. My adventurous young husband had been raised on Zane Grey's books and was more than willing to tag along. Why not go see the West?

"Honey, if we don't like it there, we can come back," Rex coaxed. Jobs were everywhere—if you wanted one—and I didn't have to live in the Midwest. The three of us, Rex, our baby Barbara, and I, could relocate easily enough.

I began to visualize a darling little home in Colorado where we could be happy and, perhaps, add to our family. So we decided to leave a good job and start on a big adventure.

Dad drove an old Reo truck with the furniture. Mom stuffed the big, passenger Velie with her most prized possessions, including her rubber plant on the seat beside her. Two extra chairs were tied on top, and a big trunk of walnuts was strapped to the back. There were sure to be no walnuts in Colorado, and there was nothing more precious to a family of good cooks than nutmeats for cookies, desserts, and breads.

Rex, Barbara, and I followed in one of our earliest family cars, a nifty Model T. My little cedar chest fit neatly between the seats, while our luggage rode strapped onto the running boards.

About the first of July in 1927, with great anticipation, our caravan headed west out of Davenport, Iowa, on the new Lincoln Highway, which was clearly marked by telephone poles with six-inch strips of red, white, and blue stripes. At the corners and crossroads along the way, we had to stop the caravan, get out, and walk up close to the poles because either the sun had faded the colors or weeds had grown up around the colored stripes.

15

Jessie and Oscar DeMoney, Vern's parents, about 1935. Oscar was a professional baker.

Jessie Isabel Brown and Oscar DeMoney in later years, about 1945. Both are buried in Rock Island, Illinois.

The first day, we drove only thirty miles because the two back tires on the overloaded truck blew out. We had to unload the Reo truck, store some of our belongings until the tire could be repaired, and then pack it again. At that time, we had no idea we were beginning a six-year odyssey of hardships. Before the Colorado years were over, money had all but vanished. Values changed, and what we once considered everyday necessities—food, clothing, shelter, and medical care—became luxuries.

No motels lined the highways then. No fast food hamburger restaurants existed. We had no ice chest or thermos to hold hot or cold refreshments. The ride for my baby Barbara was hot and rough, and it was no wonder she became cranky. We all did at times.

It took seven long days to reach Colorado. The dusty road seemed to go on and on. At many crossroads, my parents sent my younger sisters running in all directions to find our marked telephone poles or a sign, pointing the direction we should go.

Each night, we pitched our big tent in a schoolyard or court square. My mom and dad, my three teenaged sisters, Rex, Barbara, and I, all exhausted after a long day, meandered around the tent while supper cooked on a pump-up stove. Such a caravan as ours must have announced an entertainment show in town, because one old codger mistook us for the coming carnival.

"You be the show people?" he inquired of Dad, who was always willing to talk to local residents.

Dad laughed, and went on to explain that we were headed for opportunity and our new home in Colorado.

Another evening, while crossing a congested bridge over the Missouri River, the tired old Reo truck coughed, snorted, and died. Behind us, a long line of frustrated drivers on their way home from work quickly came to a halt. A traffic cop appeared almost immediately and started barking orders at us.

"Move that confounded thing off this bridge!" he said.

With a helpless gesture, Dad answered, "Mister, if you can move it, you're a better man than I am. You're welcome to get in and drive it off the bridge."

The policeman shook his head in frustration, but motioned to those behind us for assistance. Rex jumped out of the Ford and ran to help my dad and the men push, leaving me startled with the baby. The Model T Ford and I had never met on a personal basis, but I was quickly introduced. After the crippled truck limped off the bridge in front of a group of strong men, I knew that I had to do my part. I slid under the wheel of the Model T Ford, trying to remember the starting procedure. I put the clutch pedal down, then let it out in one quick motion. Jerking and lurching, Barbara and I followed our family off the bridge and out of traffic while Rex and my Dad stood laughing at me. After that first emergency lesson, I began to drive my share of the time so Rex could rest. The days slipped by after that, mostly uneventful. With heavy hearts, we discarded the chairs after they shifted perilously on the roof of the Velie. All of us were sad when the trunk of walnuts was sacrificed. Dad, a professional baker who knew its value, set it by the side of the road, hoping someone would find it and put its contents to good use.

My mother cried.

Many times in the meager years that followed, we remembered the walnuts. We often wondered about the people who found the trunk and carried it home—a whole trunk of black walnuts just sitting there on the Nebraska prairie, ready for the taking!

As we traveled, I thought of my pioneer ancestors on my mother's side of the family: Elizabeth Neal and William Hodges, Sarah Smith and Benjamin Hodges, Elizabeth Jane and John Henry Owen. There was my grandmother, Lavina Owen Brown, and her husband, John, all the way down to my mother, Jessie Isabel Brown, and my father, Oscar DeMoney (pronounced *Dee Money* with a long *O*). Each generation had been part of a pioneer journey. Each woman had done her best to keep her family well fed and healthy in a pleasant home, always working with what little she had. We weren't wealthy people, at least not when it came to money. Nevertheless, our lives were rich because we were people of faith and family.

Now it was my turn. I, too, would trek what seemed like halfway across the country, looking for a storybook life. Long before I first stepped onto the running board of the Model T, I had wanted to know about the way my predecessors had lived. I can imagine these people as if I had shared my home with them, they are so real to me. It is not because I have diaries or photographs, because there are none; but it is because my ancestors were pioneers—common people who lived off the land and worked hard—like so many people written about in history.

My story begins in Henderson County, Kentucky, in the year 1797.

FEATHER PILLOWS, CRATED CHICKENS, AND DRIED APPLES

Elizabeth Neal and William Hodges
1797-1832

Elizabeth Hodges, age twenty-one, eyed her new husband William as he swung himself up on the wagon seat beside her. She was filled with feelings of happiness, yet there were tiny shivers of excitement and fear about the new life she was about to begin. Both of their families had crossed the Cumberland Gap from Virginia, but Elizabeth and William met for the first time in Kentucky.

Henderson County was fast becoming a path for settlers from the Wilderness Road—the only road through the Cumberland Gap and over the Appalachian Mountains. Between 1775 and 1795, more than one hundred thousand pioneers surged from the east to the west by way of Cumberland Gap. In one year alone, during the late 1700s, more than twenty thousand people passed over Wilderness Road. Long before, it had become an important historical route for pioneer travelers. It wouldn't be until 1864, that General Ulysses S. Grant would inspect the same roadway from Cumberland Gap to Lexington, Kentucky.

Kentucky was the land of shuckey beans (or leatherbritches) and stack cake, where a bride's good fortune often depended on how well she could cook. Pioneer wealth then was measured in terms of family and feast. When a man died, his family and friends would "wagon the deceased to the graveyard," where everyone from the "least-uns to the grandsires loved music . . . and where dozens of other customs, including the feuding of the Hatfields and McCoys, are legendary. . . ." This was rich pioneer country.

Now Elizabeth and William were setting off on their own adventure. All summer, Elizabeth had devoted her spare time to preparations for her wedding and the life to follow. Elizabeth and her sisters had been sewing and quilting. Each Sunday after church, she and Will had lingered to quietly make plans under the shade of the oak tree in the churchyard.

Now the wagon was piled with the odds and ends they would need to start housekeeping, and Will's parents' wedding gift of a cow was tied on behind, waiting to leave. Their new cabin was just a few miles through the woods.

During fall season before the wedding, Will had worked hard harvesting his crop and raising the cabin with the help of his neighbors and family. He had chosen a particular piece of land for building his cabin because of the good spring water there. It provided a source for bathing and cleaning, as well for drinking and cooking. If there had been no spring, a well would have been dug by hand and tediously lined with stones—hard work that was time-consuming.

Elizabeth's mama had worked long days—from dawn to sundown—preparing the November wedding feast. Folks gathered early at the Neal cabin, bringing gifts of plump feather pillows to go with the new feather tick, cackling chickens in crates, dried apples, and even a pair of geese.

Sitting on the wagon seat, Will smiled at her and, putting his hand over hers, said, "We best be going. Darkness sets in early, and we must lay the fire. It gets cold in November."

Elizabeth's eyes misted as she said her farewells to friends and family. She glanced over her shoulder to once again admire the wagonload of supplies, material possessions that represented the foundation for the rest of her married life: the feather tick and pillows, quilts, dried apples, cackling chickens, a pair of geese, as well as other precious household items such as a barrel of molasses and some spices. Only the very rich could afford sugar. It came in cones wrapped in blue paper, and a special tool was needed to scrape the sugar from the cone. If one was lucky enough to acquire some, the blue paper was saved and used for dye.

She might not have sugar, but her mama had shared some of her potatoes and turnips from her summer garden to store in straw in a deep cave. They would keep most of the winter.

The leaves skittered across the yard and the cow mooed, as Will slapped the reins over the plodding old team of horses, and the young couple started off toward their new cabin. Elizabeth pulled her warm shawl closer about her against the November wind. She smoothed the folds of her blue skirt and remembered the hot day last summer when she had picked blueberries to dye the new cloth she had woven for this wedding dress.

"Wear your sunbonnet, 'lisbeth!" her mama called. "A lady doesn't let herself get too much sun."

"Yes, Mama," Elizabeth replied, smiling. She knew she would be in her own home soon, and wouldn't have to heed her mother's every direction. She looked forward to it.

In 1797, every mother wished an easier life for her daughter, but even as she called out, her mama knew that Elizabeth would soon forget about her delicate skin as she performed the hard work of a pioneer housewife. Agnes Neal looked down at her own hands, roughened from long days of toil.

It was almost dusk when the young couple came to the clearing where their cabin stood. It had one large room, no windows, and was sparsely furnished. One day, Will planned to add a window of oiled paper that would resist the rain and help keep out bugs and the cold. But for now, this would have to do. They would spend their honeymoon here, and start their new lives together.

They unloaded the wagon, making trip after trip inside the new home. Then, while Elizabeth worked inside by herself, Will carried in enough wood for the fire in the huge stone fireplace that was the focal point of their cabin. The kettle was set to boil, and Elizabeth placed her new things around the cabin. The rough pine tables and benches were ready for the couple. Her papa had carved the wooden cups and plates for her from pine, a soft wood that was easy to carve.

A bed frame built in the corner was piled high with cornhusks, and seemed to be waiting for the new feather-tick mattress and woven coverlet. Before long, pegs around the room held their few clothes, and shelves stored the lengths of hopsacking she had woven to make Will's shirts, as well as yarn to knit mittens and socks. Elizabeth was well schooled in her housekeeping chores. Every pioneer girl learned early to spin, knit, cook, and care for young children. All couples expected to have large families.

Elizabeth walked to the mantle, where she lovingly placed the Bible just as her new husband came in with an armload of wood. Their pastor had given the Bible to her after the ceremony. She looked forward to putting their names and their parents' names in it, setting down a record of her family heritage.

"Oh, Will!" she said. "This precious Bible means so much to me. Isn't it wonderful?" Few pioneer families had any books. In fact, most couldn't read.

It was Will who had transported the stones from the creek bed for the cabin's fireplace. It had a beehive oven built right in the wall. In those times, some cabins had ovens built outside, but the Kentucky winter was cold enough that it lent itself to indoor cooking, often in a big iron kettle that hung from a crane and could be swung around to hang over coals raked out on the hearth for slow cooking. Elizabeth knew it would be in constant use. At her mother's, a stew had often simmered from morning until night.

When the kettle of water boiled, Will and Elizabeth sat on sturdy benches to rest and enjoy some of the food left over from the wedding feast—thick slices of homemade bread, slabs of wild turkey, and Elizabeth's sweet molasses cake. Before they were ready to eat, they bowed their heads and clasped their hands as Will began that first blessing in their new home. "Lord, we thank you for this day and for this cabin. May it be a happy, blessed home." Elizabeth added her soft, "Amen."

In the winter that followed, William hunted, and plentiful rabbits and wild game filled the stew pot. Daily, Elizabeth cooked a stick-to-the-ribs porridge made from cornmeal for supper. Leftovers were fried in the spider, a frying pan, for breakfast along with a slab of sowbelly—fatty meat from the lower part of the sow's belly. They ate well.

Big barrels in one corner soon held their supply of cornmeal and flour. Every man took his own grain to the mill to be ground. John Neal, Elizabeth's father, had given them the snorting old sow kept in the lean-to outside, as a wedding gift. They would need to butcher her soon. She would provide meat, as well as lard and the makings for soap. Will's father (Elizabeth called him Father Hodges) had given them the cow they had led behind the wagon on their wedding day. They would keep her as long as possible for milk. When they did have to butcher her, her stomach would make rennet and her hooves would be used for gelatin.

Elizabeth knew salt licks had been found in some parts of Kentucky, and they could exchange homemade soap or eggs for salt at the fort in Boone County.

Come spring, her mama would lend them a sitting hen, and a garden would furnish the fresh produce they would need. Elizabeth knew what greens to pick for a tender, springtime treat—young dandelions, wild onions, and wild lettuce. For medicines, she had experience picking herbs such as thorn apple and skunk cabbage, which were used for treating asthma. Wild sage and honey were remedies for a baby's colic—something she didn't worry about yet, although she longed for a baby to fill her arms and their lives. May apple root and meadow cabbage served as an expectorate (to cause coughing or spitting), clearing fluids from the throat and lungs. Hemlock leaves

ROOTS AND RECIPES

and pleurisy root were medicines for the aches and pains of rheumatism.

Elizabeth Neal and William Hodges raised a large family and realized the dream of every young couple in the wilderness—to have a safe home and a loving family. One of their children was Benjamin, born in 1801.

YEAST STARTER
AND A CABIN RAISING
Sarah Smith and Benjamin Hodges
1819-1873

Benjamin Hodges was born the third of eleven children in 1801 in Harrison County, Kentucky. Like many sons of pioneers, his childhood was spent helping his father and brothers work hard in the fields and clear more land. Everyone shared in the work, and try as he might to avoid it, young Ben was no exception. Early on, he learned the meaning of hard work. What they couldn't raise themselves, the Hodges bartered for with neighbors and friends.

When Ben was almost nineteen, he noticed one pretty young woman, Sarah Smith, a widow with two small children who had migrated to Kentucky with her parents. Men often took young widows as brides, but 21-year-old Sarah was, at first, reluctant when Ben proposed to her.

"Oh, Ben," she exclaimed. "To saddle you with two children . . . Are you sure?"

Ben, anxious to leave his parents and start his own home and family, soon assured her that he loved her and the children, and wanted to be their father.

It was November 25, 1819, when Sarah and Ben were married. Neighbors and relatives brought supplies to help the new couple start housekeeping. Sarah had many of her own possessions—a feather bed, pillows, and quilts. She remembered to take yeast starter for the family's bread. Once, she foolishly forgot to save some for the next batch. That meant a long walk of many miles to a neighbor's to borrow a cupful. Baking bread was a regular chore and an important one.

Nothing was better than to enter the cabin and breathe in that aroma of fresh, hot bread.

As was the custom, all of the neighbors for miles around helped Ben raise the newlyweds' first cabin and a small barn. Whole families planned for and looked forward to the day. The women brought food to cook outside over a bonfire. Children romped and raced around the farmland with Sarah and Ben's two children. Before long, the men had the walls up. It was a great day for socializing in the otherwise plain lives of the pioneers. Everyone loved a cabin-raising!

Sarah was happy in her new home. The cabin was much like that of their parents, although a glass window was constructed early on—Sarah didn't have to wait for one like her mother-in-law had. The fireplace and her utensils were much the same. The traveling huckster, a man selling household items from his wagon or backpack, brought things they were unable to buy or trade for at the nearby fort.

Sarah knew her in-laws, Elizabeth and Will Hodges, were glad to have their son married. Of all their eleven children, they had told her they thought Ben, the third in line, was the dreamer. A wife and two children would surely inspire some ambition in him and make him settle down, they said.

Over the years, many children were born to Sarah and Ben. Although they worked from first light to dark, they were never prosperous. Ben often stood leaning on his hoe, gazing to the west. The stories he had heard of better land were hard to believe, but he dared to dream, and began to speak of it to Sarah.

"Do you suppose we could go?" he asked her. "They say some first-time settlers have moved farther west, and cabins are there just for the taking."

Hardworking Sarah, too, was convinced that something better could be just over the horizon. "I'm willing to go if you want to bad enough," she replied. It was a response that she would repeat many times in the years of their marriage, when they loaded up the wagon, tied the cow behind it, and with crates of chickens and ducks, rode away in search of what some might have thought was the golden goose. Benjamin was a wanderer, always in search of the greener grass on the other side of the hill. They moved to Indiana, then to Iowa, and back to Indiana. Sarah learned to make a new home every few years and gave birth to a houseful of babies.

One daughter, Elizabeth Jane, was born to them in late December of 1835 while they lived in Decatur County, Indiana. By then,

Sarah was thirty-seven years old. When they decided to move again—this time to Schyler County in the State of Illinois—Elizabeth Jane was old enough to help her mother pack for the journey.

This time, small fruit trees and even a favorite rose bush made the trek. These familiar, beloved landmarks of their last home made the endless moving easier for Sarah and Elizabeth Jane, too.

Although their lives may have been somewhat easier than that of earlier generations, many of the housekeeping practices were the same. Keeping a cow and a few pigs were routine for this family. Butchering time came after the first hard freeze, and good neighbors arrived early to help. Because of the lack of refrigeration, the meat was either smoked or pickled during an all-day social affair. Huge fires were started in the yard. The men worked with the hogs, and women prepared meals and shared news, gossip, and recipes.

First, Benjamin hit the hogs in the head, and a neighbor slit each hog's throat so they could be hung up to bleed. Later, Ben dunked the body in a big iron kettle of boiling water to soften the bristles—the same process as plucking chickens. Together, Ben and the neighbors scraped the skins, then cut up the meat. One of the men threw the extra fat into the big kettles to render it as lard.

All day, over a slow fire, Ben or one of the other men had to constantly stir the big pot with melting chunks of hog fat. Then the cracklings—the crisp browned skin or rind of roast pork—were drained to use in baking Johnny Cake. This cornbread dish originated in New England as white flint corn meal and water cooked on flint stones by the Indians. White settlers cooked it on griddles. This mixture also was used with dried cranberries and dried meats, such as venison. Covered wagon travelers baked the same recipe on a hoe over an open fire and called it Hoe Cake.

Sarah thought butchering day was a long, hard one, but the thought of fresh, fried pork liver for supper was a great anticipation!

From tallow, or sheep fat, Sarah loved to make candles, and the girls and youngest boys helped. Because candles were precious and used sparingly, the process for making them was a loving one. Long strips of tow, fibers removed from weaving cloth, were dipped repeatedly in hot wax. The tow was then laid over a stick to cool and harden. Some lucky pioneers had candle molds, which meant the tow was laid in the mold and the hot wax was poured over it. This was only one step beyond the primitive torches or grease lamps where a wick was laid in an open bowl.

Indian attacks were not much feared in this part of the country. Sometimes two or three fierce-looking warriors stopped at the cabin to ask for food, and Elizabeth Jane, a young pretty woman, answered the door. When she was alone, caring for the younger children while her mother worked in the garden or gathered wild berries in the woods, she still wasn't afraid. She graciously accepted the visitors and handed them a loaf of fresh bread or some cornmeal for their own cooking.

By her twentieth birthday, Elizabeth Jane had met the dashing John Owen, who was born in Licking County, Ohio, in September of 1833. He had migrated with his parents to Macomb, Illinois.

Little by little, each generation's life became a bit easier.

DILIGENT GARDENING AND JOYFUL TOE TAPPING

Elizabeth Jane Hodges and John Henry Owen
1856-1924

When John met Elizabeth Jane, my great-grandmother, he was captivated with her sparkling eyes and pleasant personality and—according to Elizabeth Jane's stories to my sisters and me—it was love at first sight. They were married in 1856 in the Hodges's home near Rushville, Illinois. Afterwards, John and Elizabeth Jane farmed for a few years, then moved to Macomb.

John was a handyman and built their home with Elizabeth Jane's help. They bought lumber from a nearby lumber mill. The plain kitchen floor, scrubbed frequently over the years, became almost white with wear and care. Elizabeth Jane had green and white dishes, and the buttermilk Majolica pitcher she used every day was one of her prized possessions that became a priceless antique and a family heirloom. Majolica was a general name for Italian earthenware glazed with a tin oxide glaze. It was generally decorated with fruits or vegetables and shaped to resemble a particular fruit or vegetable. It probably came from a traveling grocer—people sometimes called them hucksters—who went from door-to-door selling molasses, notions, spices such as cinnamon, and household supplies.

Elizabeth Jane lived in an era when she thought she was lucky.

John Owen and Elizabeth Jane Hodges Owen of Macomb,
McDonough County, Illinois.

Cook stoves with a firebox at one end were now available. A wood box stored split logs as well as kindling and corncobs to keep the fire lit. On the opposite end of the cook stove was a large reservoir to hold water for washing hair and baths in a galvanized tub. Water for cooking was heated in a tea kettle on top of the stove. A warming oven at the top of the stove kept foods until serving time, and a deep oven provided a better way of baking than the earlier conveniences. When Elizabeth Jane and John purchased their heavy, black cook stove, they took a giant step toward kitchen modernization.

Every morning, Elizabeth Jane held her hand inside the oven for one minute to test the heat. Experience told her if the oven was hot enough for baking the biscuits or muffins which were served daily for breakfast. It was a matter of pride for good cooks to be able to brag that, in all of their married years, they had never served their husbands cold "light-bread" or commercial brands for breakfast.

Like earlier generations, John and Elizabeth Jane kept a cow to provide their milk and butter, and a pig was fattened until it could be butchered in the fall. Elizabeth Jane stored the milk and butter in a pail and lowered them on a rope into the well where the cold water kept the foods from spoiling.

A large garden allowed Elizabeth Jane to amply set the table in summer. When the garden was harvested, the turnips, carrots, potatoes, and onions were stored in an outside cave for winter use. Barrels of apples from their own trees were kept crisp and sweet in winter storage as well, but not in the same place—apples release ethylene gas, which enhances sprouting of potatoes.

Wild berries and other fruits were dried or made into jams and jellies. Midwestern winters were long and hard—even the chickens must have thought so, because eggs became scarce.

Elizabeth Jane and John had a wash house built out back, where galvanized tubs hung on nails ready for use. Water had to be pumped into the tubs, then heated before clothes could be scrubbed on a washboard. Once her washtubs were set up outside the kitchen door and her homemade soap was on the washboard, Elizabeth Jane rolled up her calico sleeves and was ready to do the weekly wash. With eight children, she had plenty of help to hang their modest underthings, daily clothing, and household linens on outdoor lines to dry.

Then came the tedious job of ironing. A heavy, flat iron was heated on the stove. It took many hours of lifting the heavy iron to press clothes for their large family of ten.

In his later years, Great-grandpa John had a flowing white beard and could be found working in his garden most of the time. He pampered the rose bush with its yellow flowers until it was blooming, and the wisteria vine climbing on the outhouse was the most attractive thing you could plant to hide the unsightly and smelly building. However, the vegetable garden was more important than the flowers were to this family. John knew that when he worked, pulling weeds or thinning weak plants so that strong ones could grow, he could expect a call from his wife at the kitchen window, or out the back door.

"John! John! Bring in a head of cabbage when you come. I've got some nice sweet cream. I'll make my cabbage slaw for our dinner."

Witty and full of pep, Granny often sat on the porch in a rocker and tapped her toe while she played on her concertina and sang in a quivery little voice. We called her "Little Grandma" because she was so tiny.

In her parlor, on a marble-topped table, Elizabeth Jane kept her most prized possession: a fancy kerosene lamp. It cast light over another treasure, the family Bible.

It was easy to think of her as a vivacious housewife with eight children to raise, including a set of twins, Benjamin and Lavina, born in 1864. John and Elizabeth Jane lived together for more than sixty years. He died January 5, 1920, and she died four years later, still in Macomb, Illinois.

I was eighteen years old.

ELIZABETH JANE OWENS'S SAMPLE MENU

Cabbage Slaw
Fried Side Meat, Uncured Bacon,
or Fried Chicken with Milk Gravy
Mashed Potatoes
Buttermilk (to drink)
Pie-Plant (Rhubarb) Pie

MASHED POTATOES
WITH A LAKE OF BUTTER

Lavina Ellen Owen and John Bluford Brown
1882-1945

I can see Grandma still. She had a round face with deep-set eyes and when her family was young, she wore her hair parted in the middle. In her later years, she combed it back from her forehead in a severe hairstyle. Her hands were big, yet kind, and she was strong and stocky-looking. When she dressed up, she often wore a string of long beads and at her waist was her precious watchfob. She was tall, so we called her "Big Grandma." After all, we had called Elizabeth Jane "Little Grandma," and Lavina was a much bigger and stronger woman.

It wasn't only her size, however, that made her so different from Elizabeth Jane. Lavina Brown was a stern, strict Baptist and didn't believe in playing cards or dancing. It would have been a strange day if anyone had caught Lavina sitting on the porch, tapping her toe, and playing a concertina!

When Grandpa Brown put on a suit, he was a sight of dignity to behold. His oval face had smile lines around his eyes and the white mustache over his upper lip was like a roof over his welcoming smile. He was always lean from hard work—all of my ancestors worked with their hands—but his labor never seemed to affect his calm and easygoing disposition. He contrasted Lavina's stormy personality perfectly.

It was in 1882 that Lavina, then eighteen, met and married her carpenter beau, John Brown—not to be confused with the abolitionist John Brown who led the attack at Harper's Ferry, Virginia, in 1859. At the time of Lavina's marriage, her John was twenty-nine and a Schyler County, Illinois, native. His ancestors had migrated to Macomb from Kentucky. Lavina and John lived in the same town for their entire lives.

Most of the time Lavina wore a housedress. With her big, blue granite dishpan on her lap, she used to sit at the kitchen table, shelling new peas, separating and washing lettuce, or snapping string beans. In those days, the long string on one side had to be removed. Out back, her garden was huge and hugged the back boardwalk on both sides, producing plentiful quantities of food for canning.

Lavina's kitchen was much like her mother's: a large square room,

ROOTS AND RECIPES

Lavina Brown was a pioneer woman of dignity, faith, and femininity.

dominated on one wall by the big black cook stove with a wood box nearby. A little sink in the corner had a small pump for the cistern water, and a large pantry led from one wall where many shelves stored dishes and supplies. Against another wall was Grandma's prized kitchen cabinet. It had bins to hold the flour, sugar, and salt as well as a built-in flour sifter. How she loved that work station!

In the center of the room, a big square table was covered with a white oilcloth and decorated with salt and pepper shakers, a fresh flower from the garden when there was one in bloom, and a bowl of sugar for cereal or cinnamon toast.

Most of the family meals were eaten at this table. But like many pioneers, they used the kitchen as a family gathering place for two kinds of warmth: physical and emotional. Everything from cooking to homework was undertaken in the kitchen. Here pie crusts were rolled out, fresh-cut noodles were allowed to dry before boiling in chicken broth, and scratch cakes were mixed. Together, mothers and daughters baked cookies, cakes, pies, and breads. Preparations for holidays, happy times for families with children, were celebrated first in the kitchen.

I remember watching Big Grandma mix up her favorite angel food cakes, holding a platter on her lap and, with a steady rhythmic motion, using a wire whip to turn the egg whites into a mound of meringue. My maternal grandmother was known as a wonderful cook who produced superb meals; a good number of her recipes are part of my family collection.

I remember the Sunday dinners at her house well, when a long, snow-white linen cloth graced the huge dining room table. A silver canister held the condiments—mustard, salt, pepper, and a hot pepper sauce that Grandpa used liberally on his fried potatoes.

Without the benefit of refrigeration or a convenient stove, Lavina could make a banquet miraculously appear. From her pantry, she set the table with a variety of home-canned pickles and jams, mustard pickles, green tomato pickles, and bread and butter pickles. As a proud homemaker, Lavina boasted of the different kinds of jams and pickles she could make during the hot summer for storage in the dirt-floored cellar. In the summer, the cellar or the well were the coolest retreats and places for storage. When winter came, Lavina sent her young daughters to the shelves with instructions to bring back vegetables from the crocks or Mason jars with chunks of vegetables swimming in their sweetened or tart brine.

Grandma Brown always served two kinds of meat on Sundays or at special family dinners. Most of the time it was fried—pork chops, chicken, or ham. It was often a big roast, which was seared in the frying pan before being cooked slowly in the oven while chicken fried in crispings on the top of the black cook stove. By the time dinner was ready, mashed potatoes with a lake of butter swimming on top were served next to bowls of sweet potatoes and several kinds of vegetables. Cooked with a piece of fatty meat, they smelled and tasted so good. Even cabbage as a hot vegetable was considered unfit unless it was cooked for at least an hour with a hunk of fat meat.

Grandma defined salad as a glass dish filled with layers of sliced bananas, homemade mayonnaise, and nuts. Desserts were always the same—two kinds of pie and favorite scratch recipes of layered cake placed elegantly on a high glass plate. These were her centerpieces, which encouraged us to clean our plates!

On a truly special occasion, Grandpa John carried home a block of ice in a gunny sack to make ice cream. The salt was added and we all gathered around, watching as everyone took a turn at the crank,

Lavina Brown pictured with her husband John Brown, and children, Ruth, Edward, and Jessie (Vern's mother).

waiting impatiently with eager eyes and watering mouths for the rich milk, cream, and sugar to turn into a delicious dessert.

The birthday cakes she made were spectacular. My Uncle Ed, Jessie's brother, was a bachelor, and was babied constantly by Grandma Lavina. One time she lavishly decorated his birthday cake with pink frosting. When he came home and saw it, he complained, "You know I don't like pink frosting." By the time the cake came to the table, it was more masculine-looking with a thick chocolate topping. Underneath, there was a layer of pink, which everyone politely ignored, including Uncle Ed.

The high-calorie, greasy diet of early Americans didn't make for fat people in Lavina's day. They worked too hard, not only with their hands, but with their backs. Water had to be pumped from the well outside the back door or from a pump that provided cistern water collected during a soft rain for baths and shampoos.

A neat and tidy child on Sundays was one whose parents loved him or her, and Lavina was a good mother. She routinely laundered clothes on a worn washboard, then hung them out in the fresh air to dry. She labored over ironing, using flat irons heated on the stove, so that handkerchiefs, sheets and pillowcases, as well as her family's clothes, appeared fresh and cared for. But the work never seemed to end. Any excess calories after such chores were surely worked off with garden work and scrubbing floors on hands and knees.

In Grandma and Grandpa Brown's parlor, there was an organ. This room was off-limits to us unless there was company—and we were family, not company. Besides, we were too little for this adult social place.

The organ, too, required energy, but this was a pleasant kind: pumping the foot pedals and playing the black and white keys. I don't ever remember Grandma Lavina or Grandpa Brown playing, it was more of a status symbol to own one. We girls took piano lessons and tried to play exercises.

Of all my sisters, Thelma—we called her Jerry—and I were closest. We were teenagers together and used to spend a few weeks each summer with Grandpa and Grandma Brown. When our strict Baptist grandmother asked questions about our parents' social life, we were primed by my mother to politely change the subject, while avoiding outright lies.

"Do your mama and papa go to dances?" she asked.

"Well, they go to the Moose Lodge, but I don't know what they do there," I'd say, my cold hands in my lap. I don't remember if I could meet her eyes, but I do remember wishing she wouldn't ask me such questions.

I didn't see anything wrong with dancing or having a good time. I, too, loved to dance. One summer, a girlfriend named Alvera went with me to visit Grandma and Grandpa. The people across the street had a wind-up Victrola and a daughter our age. We went to visit one evening. As the music played, I taught Alvera and our new friend how to dance. Grandma saw us from the porch swing.

When we came home it was after dark, and we immediately knew that she was angry with us. She hadn't left any lights on for us, and she hadn't laid out the folding bed we slept on each night. But we didn't care. We giggled and laughed as we entered the house. Once Alvera was asleep, I stared into the dark, listening to my friend's breathing. I thought about the terrific scolding I would surely have to bear in the morning. Tossing and turning, I finally fell asleep.

But Big Grandma surprised me by never saying a word. Her message was more subtle. At the breakfast table, lying next to my plate was a book, *From the Ballroom to Hell.*

The parlor was the warmest and prettiest room in the house—not in terms of temperature, because during the winter it was cold. But it served as a welcoming place for important guests and neighbors, as well as for formal family gatherings. I thought the parlor was a pretty room because, like many ancestral homes, treasured family heirlooms were safest from young hands when kept in the off-limits room. It was a placed filled not only with prized possessions, but precious family love.

Hand-woven rugs of strips of fabric covered the floor in that room, and white lace curtains covered the windows. The stiff lace curtains were regularly taken down, washed and starched, then stretched on a curtain stretcher. Each spring and fall, a special tool was used to loosen the tacks holding the carpet. It was hauled outdoors, thrown over the clothesline, and beaten with a wire carpet-beater until the dust flew no more. Before the carpet was replaced and secured, fresh straw was scattered over the floor. No wonder people in Lavina and John Brown's generation didn't count calories!

At the back of the family lot, a pig was kept for winter butchering, and a big chicken house and yard were filled with a rooster and hens that provided eggs. When Lavina said so, chickens were also butchered to eat. I chased them all over the yard until I caught a squawking hen, then turned the poor thing over to Mama, Grandma, or Grandpa, and I watched as her neck was stretched across a stump and a broom handle put on top. One of them stepped on both sides of it. Pulling on the hen's feet eventually separated the body and head. The body was tossed to the side, and it flopped all over the yard until there was no life left. It was an awful sight, and I hated to watch it, but I knew, even as I helped pluck feathers with the smell of singed flesh in boiling water offending my nose, that it was a necessary chore. It would all be forgotten once we smelled the aroma of Sunday's frying chicken—and even more so when we tasted the chicken, mashed potatoes, and gravy.

In her later years, Grandma Brown's house was wired with electricity, replacing the kerosene lamps. She never knew the joy of a modern stove or a refrigerator, but I doubt that she complained. She wasn't the complaining kind. Stern and strict, yes, but not complaining.

As for me, I am still reluctant to sew on Sunday because of Lavina's influence on me. As we grew up, Big Grandma assured us over and over that we would pay for such a sin. She used to say to us, "You will have to pick the stitches out with your nose when you get to Heaven!"

John and Lavina lived hard but productive lives. They had five children, and it was a source of great sorrow when two died in infancy. My mother, Jessie Isabel Brown, was their firstborn on May 17, 1883.

LAVINA BROWN'S SAMPLE MENU

Cucumbers and Onions (in season)
Various Condiments (in winter)
Fried Chicken and Roast Beef or Baked Ham
Mashed Potatoes with Milk Gravy
Sweet Potatoes in Brown Sugar Syrup (when available)
Green Beans Cooked with Bacon (in summer)
Corn on the Cob (in summer) or Canned Corn (in winter)
Homemade Bread and Butter
A Tall Cake on a Stand—probably Angel Food Cake
(for which she was famous)
Two Kinds of Pie—Vinegar or Apple
Fresh Fruits

THE BAKER AND JESSIE BROWN
Jessie Isabel Brown and Oscar DeMoney
1905-1950

Oscar DeMoney, a Missouri native, was an adventurous young man. He was born in Bible Grove in Scotland County, Missouri, and grew to adulthood there. He left a steady job and drifted, working as a baker in a bake shop or as a hired hand so that he might see more of the United States. He went by covered wagon to Kansas, working with horses and doing farm chores along the way. He rode the rails to the state of Washington, where his earlier bakeshop training led him to cooking in bars where free lunches were served to drinking customers.

When he was twenty-five years old, he decided his roaming days were over. He settled in Macomb, Illinois, where he worked in a bakery and soon met a customer, brown-haired Jessie Brown. They were married in Macomb in 1905. As the years passed, four daughters

Vern DeMoney with her sister Thelma, about 1909. Many early pioneer families did not have resources for such luxuries as cameras and film, particularly during the Depression.

Vern and Thelma, 1910.

were born to this couple; I came first, a year later, in 1906. My sisters followed: Thelma (we called her Jerry), Ruth (Rusty), and Irene, now my only living sister.

When I was a young girl, the kitchen was the center for most of our daily activities. It had a linoleum floor, a white oilcloth-covered table, and an oak ice box that was my mother's pride and joy. She placed a card in the front window as a signal to the delivery man that we needed ice. When he drove by, he stopped with his team of horses in front of the house, yelling, "Whoa!" He got down, walked to the back, and opened the canvas curtain of the wagon. Using ice tongs, he lifted a block of ice to his leather-padded shoulder, then carried it into the house where he placed it in the zinc-lined portion of the oak box. It kept food from spoiling for long periods of time, but sometimes, when we forgot to empty the pan of melted ice water that was hidden underneath, it overflowed onto the floor! If it was my assigned chore, and I forgot, I was the first to be on my hands and knees, mopping up the water.

On one wall of the kitchen, opposite the ice box, there was a kerosene stove with a modern built-in oven. A pantry, much like Grandma Lavina's, held supplies and dishes. Outside in the yard, a large garden produced the vegetables for summer meals. New peas or sweet corn were a once-a-year delicacy. Mama used to get angry when we'd eat so many tender peas before she could get them to the table. There were no frozen foods like we have today available for year-round enjoyment. So we helped Mom can pints and quarts of produce from the garden for winter meals: tomatoes, tomato juice, green beans, corn, peas, and pickles. It wasn't so different from Grandma's day—except for our meat. We didn't have to butcher it ourselves because by this time, meat was purchased from a butcher shop—a cool clean store with sawdust on the floor and, behind the counter, a butcher block table where meats were cut and trimmed to order.

My fifth birthday is one year I'll never forget because we delivered invitations to my friends by horse and buggy.

"Sit quietly, and don't muss your dress," Mama said as we rode behind the horse. My mother was a quiet, gentle lady, who felt it was important to make a good impression. She held the reins easily, though I later learned she always feared driving the horse and buggy.

"Yes, Mama," I said politely. "Where are we going next?"

I don't remember her answer, but from house to house we went.

There were about ten in all. Now, more than eighty years later, I don't remember much about that party. The most important thing seemed to be helping Mama deliver the invitations.

Even though we ate good homemade food at our house, I remember how thrilling it was for me to visit Dad's bakery in Macomb. Big ceiling fans stirred the air, and delicious smells met me at the door. To stand in front of the glass case and pick a treat was wonderful. Big, fat cookies or sweet oozing fancy cream puffs made decision-making difficult.

In 1911, when I was five years old, our family moved to Davenport, Iowa. We rented a duplex, a two-unit house; these were very popular at the time. At first, my dad worked at Krell's Party Supply House, a bakery where he created towering wedding cakes and fancy sweets for the local clientele.

About nine years later, my parents bought the Mt. Ida Bakery at 1230 East 12th Street in Davenport, and Dad finally had his own business. It was located in what was known as the Mt. Ida area of Davenport, at 12th Street and College Avenue, where a church and a drugstore are now located. My sisters and I were raised around bakery goods—both in the bakeshop and the family home. Despite the possibility of providing for our table from my father's shop, my mother stubbornly insisted on baking the pies and cakes for our own table.

My mother had her own version of strawberry shortcake—a special family favorite—that she made with a traditional white layer cake. She spread it with seven-minute frosting and placed whole berries between the layers. On top, she lavished frosting and the red, plump fruit. From my mother-in-law, I learned that some people eat shortcake that looks like rich, sweet biscuits.

Although my mother was unlike her mother, Lavina, in that she loved to dance and saw no harm in it, my mother clung to her domestic teachings. She prepared many dishes by frying, and used cream and butter lavishly. She also taught us to sew.

In those days, pantywaists, bloomers, and petticoats, as well as dresses and pinafores, were made at home. Our dresses were always special, with lots of tucks and ruffles. The sewing machine was in the dining room, with an open door into the bakery, so mother could sew when she wasn't serving customers. Many times when I came home from school, her voice would greet me with a task.

"Now, Vernadine, you can pick up the scraps and tie all the threads."

I groaned. We all appreciated the nice clothes, but I didn't like the boring job of knotting threads.

Then Mom would call to Jerry, and a smile would cross my face.

"Jerry, honey, the dining room has to look nice for supper. Close the machine and set the table."

While we were still little, Mama made dresses alike for Jerry and me. Our good dresses one winter were the envy of all our friends: high-waisted blue serge pleated skirts with matching short blue velvet jackets trimmed at the neck with white ermine fur. We learned quite early that we could have more clothing if we made it ourselves.

On the back porch of my childhood home, a wooden tub washing machine, used to clean all of our pretty and everyday things, was operated by hand power. Water still had to be pumped and heated, then transferred to the washing machine. Someone—usually me because I was the oldest—pushed the lever back and forth to make it work.

Keeping clothes clean and being clean in general were hard work in those days.

So that we could look our best, Mama washed our hair with rain water before tying it up in rags. A necessary amount of water was dipped out of the rain barrel carefully, avoiding the gnats which always gathered on top. Then one of us carried it into the kitchen and poured it into the reservoir for heating on the cook stove. When it was time, each of us took our turn, bending over the sink or a tub for the bar soaping and smelly vinegar rinse.

It was a painful ordeal to have my long hair "done up in rags." Mama carefully combed out the tangles (there were no cream rinses then), and parted my hair off in sections. Holding a long strip of a rag close to my head, she wound the hair around and around the end, then wrapped the leftover rag back up around the cork screw curl to the top and tied a knot. I had to sleep in the rags, and it seemed to take my hair forever to dry.

Mama always towel-dried her own hair. In good weather she sat in the sun until all dampness had disappeared. She heated a crimpy-looking curling iron in the top of a lamp chimney and frizzed the front in a frame around her face. Today when I see young girls on the street or at the grocery store who have crimped their hair, I wonder why, when there are so many other modern conveniences.

When I was about ten, I came down with diphtheria and had to be quarantined in an upstairs bedroom. The doctor was mystified. I was the only patient diagnosed in the then so-called Tri-Cities area (Davenport, Iowa, and Rock Island and Moline, Illinois), and he couldn't figure out where I had contracted it.

My father, whose occupation made it even easier to spread a contagious disease, had to stay away from me and from home. Along with all of her other duties, my mother became my only nurse. Whether being a wife, mother, seamstress, housekeeper, or nurse to a very sick little girl, she was always sweet, cheerful, and slow to anger. Dozens of times a day, I would call to her.

"Mama, bring me a drink," or "Mama, please read to me."

"Coming, Vernadine," she would call up the stairs. Each time she left me, she had to wash herself with disinfectant and change her clothes before going downstairs, so she wouldn't carry the disease to my sisters.

In Davenport, our kitchen had more modern conveniences—a gas stove and mantle lights on the wall. A pay gas meter in the basement gobbled up our precious quarters. Besides remembering to empty the water pan from under the oak ice box, we had to think about feeding the quarter meter before a baking project. If we didn't, the gas would run out and our cakes would fall.

Like Grandma Brown, my mother Jessie often baked biscuits for breakfast. She served them with milk gravy, bacon, and eggs. A spoonful of flour was added to the bacon drippings, then cold milk. She stirred the gravy until it began to boil and became thick and rich—and fattening, by today's standards.

Every Sunday, my mom concocted a fruit salad which she made with Jell-O, bananas, and oranges. Frequently on Saturdays, she sent one of us to the butcher shop for a ring of homemade liver sausage and bologna. That would be our supper along with soup and crackers.

Jerry, Rusty, Irene, and I started early to help Mom in the kitchen. She insisted we all learn to be good cooks. As the oldest, I began cooking at a very young age, and discovered I liked fixing food.

One time my Uncle Alvin, my dad's brother, and his new wife were stopping by for dinner. It was a time of great excitement—meeting a new bride. At the last minute, Mom developed one of her wicked headaches. Those headaches always put her to bed, so I was charged with preparing the meal.

Back and forth, up and down the stairs, I ran to my mother's bedside for explicit instructions. Without her coaching, I never would have accomplished the task. But she felt terrible for being forced to leave such a job to one so young as me.

"I'm so sorry, honey." She actually cried. But I felt grown up and important—almost as important as when I sat next to her on the buggy seat, delivering those invitations. I don't remember a single thing I served, except for the white cake I made and frosted, then topped with fresh strawberries. Many years later, my Aunt Marian remarked, "How Jessie taught her girls to cook and what a fine dinner Vernadine served—with directions from upstairs!"

By the time I was twelve, I began going through my own feminine generation's type of rebellion. I loathed the high-topped, laced shoes and long underwear I always wore, and begged my parents for a pair of the new stylish oxfords. My Dad eventually bought the shoes, but he refused to relent on the issue of long underwear. So every morning, I put them on, walked part-way to school, then stopped to roll up the underwear, tucking it under the elastic of my bloomers. My legs were no longer covered, but the bulky fabric created a big lump on the side. Nevertheless, I wasn't the only girl my age who looked extra "hippy."

In 1925, at the age of nineteen, I married a wonderful man named Rex. We lived together for fifty-one years until the day he died.

JESSIE DEMONEY'S SAMPLE MENU

Fruit Salad—Often Gelatin with Bananas and Oranges

Stewed Chicken and Dumplings, Homemade Noodles

Mashed Potatoes and Gravy

Homemade Rolls or Cinnamon Rolls

Canned Corn or Green Beans with Bacon

Hickory Nut Cake or Fruit Pie (in season), such as Grape Pie

WESTWARD IN THE VELIE
AND MODEL T FORD
Vernadine DeMoney and Rex Berry
1925-

When I met Rex Berry, he was tall and thin, and lived nearby. Later, he worked in a Studebaker car manufacturing factory in South

Bend, Indiana. He was visiting in Davenport, and came into the Mt. Ida Bakery that my father owned and where I worked.

Even before we were married on May 24, 1925, I began cooking all of Mom's specialties in an attempt to put some fat on him. While I sat across the table, watching him eat, I sampled my own cooking, which didn't help my weight a bit. I was a good cook even then, and over the years, my love for the art continued to increase my skills.

Rex and I first lived in a small apartment in South Bend, Indiana. It had a gas stove and an ice box. I had to share an old hand-operated washing machine with the other tenants, but we did have electric lights, as did my folks who were living in Davenport, Iowa.

One of my very first recipes—that didn't come from my mother— was a gift from a new bride who lived across the street from us. She called it creamed hamburger. It has been a life-long recipe. You can stretch it as far as needed, and my two little girls, Barbara and Doris, loved it. During World War II's rationing days, it helped make a small amount of meat go a long way.

In 1927, my family made the move by Model T, Velie, and old Reo truck caravan to Bennet, Colorado, a small town thirty-five miles straight east of Denver. My father's health was failing, and my parents thought they could sell the bakery and buy a ranch where the climate might be better, near where my dad's brother Virgile lived. Of course, they wanted Rex and me to go with them. We decided to try it, telling ourselves that if we didn't like it, we could always return to Iowa.

We started out on the long journey with high hopes, expecting to make a good life under Colorado's big sky. I couldn't help remembering my ancestors' adventure back in 1797, when Elizabeth and William Hodges were perched atop the wagon seat, riding toward a new life in the wilderness. When we left, I wondered if Elizabeth had felt as I did then—jittery, yet full of anticipation and excitement. It was a painful, miserable journey. Flat tires, truck breakdowns, and sacrificed possessions—the trunk of walnuts and chairs tied on top— seemed to mark the miles from Iowa westward.

When the mountains began to show like low clouds on the horizon in Colorado, we started to look for a sign nailed to a post and pointing south: Twenty Miles to Bennet. There we turned, meandering across the unfenced fields, startling the thousands of prairie dogs back into their holes and avoiding the cactus growth in the little-used car or truck tracks. We felt such relief to be so close to our destination.

Seven, long, hot, dusty days had finally brought us there. At last, our great dream could begin.

We were soon to learn that a big disappointment awaited us. There was no house to rent. My Uncle Virgile, a weathered old homesteader, greeted us with the news. "Now folks, you'll just be coming in with us till something turns up."

His big heart allowed us to move in with him and his wife. They had a four-room, rough-lumber house. It was all he had needed some years earlier to earn his homestead. My aunt took the extra roommates in stride. She dressed an extra chicken or two from her barnyard of hens and doubled up the recipe for the cornmeal mush she served for supper. This was one of my first lessons in true hospitality.

Dad and Rex were not to be discouraged. In the days that followed, they borrowed two cookshacks from the county, hauled them into the dooryard, and placed them side by side, cutting a door from one to the other. I tried not to let the disappointment show on my face as I remembered the home we left back in Iowa.

For hours before moving in, we scrubbed the ugly floors with their wide boards. Actually living there was something else. The tarpaper roof sizzled under the summer sun, and the big black cookstove made the temperature almost unbearable. There was no point in unpacking my cedar chest here. Nice things didn't belong.

Shortly after we arrived, it was wheat harvest time. Uncle Virgile, Dad, and Rex used the truck to haul wheat from the fields to the big elevators. The men had quickly adjusted to this new life, delighting in the work under the big blue sky. Early every morning, they drove away, following the big threshing machines. At noontime, they enjoyed dinners prepared by the prairie farmwives. Even the old truck took a new lease on life. It seemed to chug away happily in this new role. Rex, Dad, and Uncle Virgile came home at supper time, tired and dirty, with pay for the day's work. After supper, they cut up fuel for the monstrous, wood-gobbling cookstove.

Life was discouraging for Mom and me. Most of the time, it was miserably hot. The sun bore down on the tarpaper roof and made cooking and baking nearly impossible. There was no shade from trees anywhere, and no ice for cooling lemonade or tea. We were used to Iowa, where flowers graced the landscape, and trees towered over the healthy green soybeans and corn. To say it mildly, the transition to our new home was difficult.

We had to carry water in for cooking, cleaning, and bathing, then carry it back out after use. We washed clothes on a board in a tub outside. We had to heat irons for pressing clothes on the stove. The cycle of work never ended. Washing, then ironing for the eight of us, then starting all over again. There were no pretty curtains and no closets. Our things hung on nails around the shack. We had no bathroom; we shared my aunt and uncle's outhouse. My pretty belongings waited in the dark cedar chest. Sometimes I opened the lid and admired what I had brought for our dream home in the West, and wondered if I'd ever get to use them again.

My sisters soon adapted to prairie life. There were plenty of boyfriends who came to squire them to weekly dances. Picnic trips to the mountains or a day in Denver made for an exciting summer for them. Mom and I stayed home, struggling to keep some kind of a home without the comforts we had before. The sky was so blue, and the clouds were so dreamy and fluffy white. Where was our little dream house in the West?

One bright day, with healthy, golden wheat waving ripe and ready, a sudden angry sky and wind appeared. In an instant, devastating hail left only a stubble of grain to taunt the heartsick farmers. Now there was no wheat left to haul. But that wasn't all the hail did to us that day. The tarpaper roof, riddled with holes, wasn't much protection from the torrents of rain that followed. My young sisters, close to being hysterical, laughingly raised an umbrella and sat huddled in the middle of a bed to escape the rain dribbling through the roof. It's true about the old saying, "Laughter is next to tears."

During the storm, a crock of bread dough waited on the back of the stove and bean soup simmered for supper. After the hail and rain had stopped, Mom calmly made out the pan biscuits while I tried to clean up the mess. As we ate our meal, the mountains shimmered with a beautiful haze in the distance, but we didn't enjoy the sight. Despair, worry, and disappointment etched our faces as we sat around the table.

Not long after that, however, Rex came hurriedly into the shack with exciting news. "Honey, I'm going to work for the Ford garage. And besides that, I found a little empty house on the edge of town, too."

Joy of joys! Hand in hand, we looked at the little box of a house. Nothing could have ever been so beautiful to me. Suddenly life was fun again. We bought a kerosene stove that had a little oven to set on the top burners. There was a small drop-leaf table for the kitchen, and we borrowed a chair and a rocker. With money from our dwindling savings, we bought dishes and pans.

The little cracker box Rex and I moved into was a haven of privacy after that long, hot summer of living with so many family members. Unpacking my pretty things was such a treat, and getting acquainted with neighbors made me feel like a new bride. Learning to cope with scarce commodities in the little town, however, was something that took getting used to.

There were no rows of colorful vegetables to choose from at Nye's Market, only tins of tomatoes, corn, or peas. Smoked meats and canned salmon or sardines were the only choices for meat. Cookies and crackers were offered in bulk displays. Bolts of dry goods stood on one shelf, and I can't remember seeing pop or anything to drink like there was back home. Plenty of milk and farm eggs were available; however, my folks had settled on a nearby sharecrop ranch and they kept us well-supplied.

One Sunday, a carload of people drove into our yard just at mealtime. It seems that the custom in Bennet was that if you didn't go visiting, a family came to your house—unannounced.

"Come in," I called out, wondering what to feed them.

"We came to make you welcome!" the sun-weathered woman said. "Are you home today?"

"Yes, we're home today," I said, wracking my brain for what I could put together.

There were only cans of salmon, kidney beans, and peaches on my pantry shelf. It didn't take long to make a salmon loaf and I had made kidney-bean salad many times before. But the big hit of the meal was the warm biscuit shortcake topped with canned peaches.

"I never heard of peach shortcake!" the lady said. Well, neither had I. But I quickly learned to improvise and substitute, or do without. That was the blueprint for survival in those early Depression years. To keep pride and dignity in your homemaking, with little available help, needless to say, was a challenge.

Before long, I heard from another woman that I'd been marked as one of Bennet's good cooks. Out on those desolate plains, I thought that was quite an achievement, and I felt proud.

In our little town, we made our own entertainment. There was neither television nor radio. The men played softball, while the women visited and talked over family events or shared recipes. In the winter, we spent hours playing cards. We gathered books and started a lending library. How wonderful it was to spend the dark hours beside a brightly burning mantle lamp and lose oneself in a good book.

The big event of the week was the Saturday night dance. (We didn't write home to Big Grandma Lavina about it!) It cost one dollar to dance to the music of a live Denver band. At midnight, a lunch was served. Whole families attended with children sleeping on benches that lined the walls. The little towns were thirty to forty miles apart, and whole communities shifted from one place to another to dance to "My Blue Heaven" and "Sleepy Time Gal" on Saturday night.

Church services were held in the schoolhouse. The straight-laced preacher frowned on dancing, so his congregation was small. Living was frugal after the hailstorm, and people needed that night of frivolity. They actually lived by the Golden Rule in their everyday dealings. Each man shared and helped his neighbor. This was our Code of the West.

By springtime, the Great Depression had slowed everything to a halt. Mother and I were determined to have flowers, and we carried buckets and buckets of water. But the seeds we planted in the spring were blown from the ground as fast as we planted them. Not a seed grew to produce color or fragrance, and I longed for the rich Iowa soil.

The desperate ranchers planted and replanted seeds, only to have them blown away in a fury. The brown rolling clouds of dust sent everyone for cover. Relentlessly, for three days at a time, the wind swirled and blew dust and tumbleweeds against fences until no fences remained. The wind ruined everything in its path.

Under such living conditions, it was most difficult to fix a variety of meals. I learned all over again how to feed my family by substituting and improvising, this time on next to nothing for ingredients. When I thought of Elizabeth and William, and even my mother's mother whom I still remember so well, I couldn't imagine that they had less to work with than I did then.

Knowing that life in those days depended upon hard work and careful planning for the bitter winter months, we began using the barter system to survive. No one had money to pay for the repairs Rex made in the little business he had started for himself. So he traded work for whatever was available in someone else's barnyard or pantry. Chickens and home-butchered meat were welcomed trades. So were potatoes, milk, and eggs. One time, a trucker paid his bill with a bushel of sweet potatoes. We thought they were a gift from heaven! I fixed them in every possible way. Whenever I had a chicken, I invented ways to make it look and taste different. If I had flour and a neighbor had eggs, we made a cake together and shared it. When the spice or pepper can was empty, there was no more to fill them. We learned to make do with what we had.

Coffee was only twenty-five cents a pound, but when we had such a luxury, we restricted its use to breakfast. The smell of fresh-brewed coffee lasted longer through the day when started early.

In my spare time, I sewed dresses for Barbara from castoffs until the last sewing machine needle broke. I can't describe the helpless, hopeless feeling of knowing that once something like that was gone; there was no replacing it.

It is still strange to me, but the Christmas when we had no money to spend on gifts or special food is the one I remember the most vividly and happily in my long married life. We used a tumbleweed for a Christmas tree, and I made little popcorn balls to hang with bits of yarn. Barbara's eyes lit up with joy when she saw the doll clothes I had sewn from scraps of cloth and the bed made from a simple box. No little girl was ever more thrilled.

Writing to friends and relatives back home had to stop during those years. There was no cash for three-cent stamps. No one had a dollar for a dance anymore. Even the blue Colorado sky had turned to murky brown most of the time. I began to long for the Saturday night dances and the fun I felt we young people should have been enjoying.

Even in bad times, life and love go on and somehow grow stronger. When I learned I was pregnant again, we couldn't imagine where we could find the money to pay a doctor. Maybe things would get better, we told ourselves. Other people had babies. Then I had an idea.

"Rex, do you think we could risk holding a dance? Would people come? Maybe we could earn enough to pay the doctor," I said.

Anyone could put on a dance. All we had to do was rent a hall and hire a band. But the band alone would cost $50. We decided to take a chance. We rented the school gym and hired a group of musicians. What if no one came? No one suspected that I was expecting. Pregnant ladies didn't discuss such things, and they certainly didn't organize social events or go to dances!

When the big night arrived, people came in droves, and I breathed a prayer of gratitude. Our spirits rose with the happy tunes and laughter rang from the throats of worry-ridden neighbors. Late that night, we counted the stacks of silver dollars that would pay for bringing our baby, Doris, into the world. Weeks later, right on time, and with the help of the old country doctor, our red-headed, ever-screaming second daughter came into our lives. It was as though she hated the world. Nothing seemed to agree with her. While we tried every available food, including goat's milk from a sympathetic neighbor, we watched her grow thinner. No pediatrician was near. Only a mother's arms night and day, and the final resort of feeding her crumbled toast and soft egg, finally got her on the way to being a sweet little daughter.

Periodically, the dust storms continued. To be caught in one was like driving in a blizzard of pure dirt. No grass surrounded the houses. No flowers or trees would grow. The fields were still dormant—seeds blew out faster than they could be planted. We began to think of giving up and going home—if we could scratch together money for the trip.

Then came Roosevelt and the New Deal. His fireside chats gave us hope. We yearned for the green grass and trees of Iowa. We huddled where there was a radio and discussed the upheavals in Washington. The dust storms kept coming. Roosevelt couldn't stop them with any program. We realized that prosperity would come to the eastern states first. For six years, we struggled, made do, made over, or did without.

The years in Colorado were hard and filled with disappointments and failures. Many people lost their homes or ranches. Nothing is as sad as a deserted farm home with empty windows, like sad eyes. We missed Iowa and decided home sweet home was where we wanted to be. In 1933, Rex, the girls, and I drove away and left our repair shop. Destitute, but not defeated, we turned the Ford to the east, with the cedar chest between the seats and our two little girls in front. I sat in back because a window was broken out.

My parents followed a few weeks later.

At first, we moved in with Rex's sister, who lived in Pleasant Valley, Iowa, near the Mississippi River. She had a basement full of home-canned foods. When I first walked before those shelves filled with sweet corn, green beans, tomatoes, and strawberry jam, I couldn't wait to help with the cooking.

Rex found employment with Farmall, an agricultural implement manufacturer, that same year. His first check for a week's work was $17.50. It was so much money that I didn't know what to do with it. We had been without for so long, I couldn't think who or what to spend it on. Should I buy a winter coat for Barbara? Doris needed shoes. There were so many things we needed.

The men hunted that winter, and the rabbits and squirrels they provided for the pot fed us until spring. By the time we found our own apartment, Barbara, six, was in second grade. Doris, about three, was still home with me. As the years went by, Rex rose to the position of superintendent and stayed with the company for thirty-five years.

Every year, as the girls grew older, our lives became easier. It also seemed easier to cook better. Kellogg's Corn Flakes, marketed in 1906, was the first dry cereal. I rolled my chicken in the crushed flakes and my family thought it was tasty. Bisquick was the very first baking mix. It was introduced in 1931, and I soon learned to use it for a variety of main dishes and breads. Cake mixes, on the grocery store shelves in 1940, bothered me at first—I was so used to cooking from scratch that I couldn't imagine a good boxed cake mix. I still had my copy of the very first cookbook, published in 1742. It was called *The Competent Housewife,* and included household hints and home remedies. Most early housewives didn't have cookbooks; they couldn't read. But that didn't stop them from trading recipes and remembering.

We bought a house in Davenport in 1938, but it was 1945 before I had my first electric refrigerator. When Rex began having migraine headaches, we thought they were because of his work. We decided to move and buy a business, Berry Motor Company, in Tipton, Iowa. Rex sold and repaired small engines and equipment for farmers.

It was then that I started entering contests, using my writing skills to win prizes. I won my first all-modern electric stove in a Pillsbury Bake-Off Contest in 1954, and soon I became a contest fanatic. Rex laughed at me—until I won the trip to—of all places—Cuba in 1957, the year before Castro came to power.

The contest was to write in twenty-five words or less why I liked a pair of pliers. So I told Rex to go to the hardware store and look at them, then tell me what was different about them. I wrote it as if I were Rex, and started it: "Forty years as a mechanic . . ." I compared the "multi-pliers" to others, using a comparison of dog pedigrees. I think the line that won was: "Pedigree promises enduring service." When Mr. Poluska, the man whose company sponsored the contest, called from Chicago, I was terrified to meet him. I decided to tell him the

Vern Berry, number 24 and one of one hundred finalists in the
Pillsbury Bakeoff at the Waldorf Astoria in 1954. *Photo by Ted Bates
& Company.*

truth: that Rex hadn't written the entry, I had. Mr. Poluska came to
Tipton and met us at the hardware store, where the owners shared the
prize as retailers for the pliers.

"I have to tell you," I said nervously. "Rex didn't write that entry,
I did." I held my breath and waited, expecting that he'd disqualify us
on the spot.

Instead, the man looked at me and grinned.

"I don't give a damn who wrote it," he said. "It was good, and it
is the winning entry. We're going to use what you said in national
advertising, and you're going to Cuba."

They took us to Des Moines and sent us on to New Orleans for a
few days before we went on to Cuba. On the way back, we flew
through Miami. It was a dream vacation!

In 1976, when I was seventy years old and after fifty-one years of
marriage, Rex died of lung cancer. My whole world fell apart. I sold
our house and moved to a high-rise apartment for the elderly in Bettendorf, Iowa. I wanted to be near my daughters.

My relocation was trying: I had to find a new church, bank, and doctor, and go shopping in unfamiliar places. Old friends who were still couples drifted away, and it is hard to make new friends when you're in your seventies. I was left to scratch around for new entertainment, so I cooked big family dinners, gave brunches for widowed friends, or went out to eat.

I was so lonely, I jumped to sign up for a writer's conference at a college nearby that I had heard about on television. When I won an award as the most promising unpublished writer at the conference, I really perked up. I came home, dug out some old stuff I'd written years before, and sent it off to publishers. At first, I received rejection letters, but with practice and help from writing friends, I began to sell and see my work in magazines and newspapers such as *Kitchen-Klatter, Weight Watchers,* and *American West.* Most were nostalgia pieces or related to cooking. Each time I received an acceptance letter, the publication of my life experiences was more rewarding than the money, but I didn't complain about cashing the checks!

It was surprising to me when I started receiving invitations to speak at church and social clubs. People told me they had heard about my writing—I didn't start until I was seventy—and they wanted to hear more about my work.

Now, as a great-grandmother, I'm in my late eighties and I still love to cook and write when I can. Church is still important to me, and with friends, I often enjoy someone else's cooking after the service. When I'm asked to bring something for a potluck meal, those who know me often request my special home-baked bread or rolls. After one of my recipes was published in a holiday cookbook, a lady called to tell me she had sent her California-based daughter a batch of the cookies. Her daughter called long-distance for the recipe.

Recently, I entered another baking contest. All five recipes were considered semi-finalists for the baking competition! When the newspaper editor called to suggest that I limit my entries to two or three because each recipe needed to be prepared for the tasting contest, I chose two and won with my Baked Christmas Candy.

My marriage to Rex was blessed and filled with memories that I treasure to this day. If I were to tell anyone what I've enjoyed most in recent years, it's this new and exciting journey into the unknown. Although Elizabeth Hodges may have enjoyed sitting in the rocker on the front porch, tapping her toe and playing a concertina, it's not the life for me.

I like to keep moving.

It has been almost two hundred years since Elizabeth and Will set up housekeeping. We have progressed from fireplace cooking, kerosene stoves, and the big fired cook stoves, to today's modern ranges and microwaves; and from trading posts and hucksters who supplied our household needs to huge supermarkets. Refrigerated trucks and planes move foods around the world. We no longer depend on home gardens and home butchering for fresh produce and meat.

Now, at the time of this writing, I am in my late eighties, and I have seen many of these changes myself. I can't help but wonder what awaits our future homemakers. No matter what develops, women through the ages, cooking and caring for their families with any available means, will be unsung heroines in the developing history of this land.

VERN BERRY'S SAMPLE MENUS

Brunch

Frozen Fruit and Topping
Party Scrambled Eggs or Sour Cream Quiche
Orange Kiss-Me Rolls
Clothes Pin Spins or Coffee Cake Variation
Plenty of Coffee

Dinner

Tossed Salad with Mandarin Oranges
Oven-Fried Chicken
Fancy Potato Bake
Dilly Green Beans
Potato Dinner Rolls
Graham Cracker Meringue Dessert

It was impossible to plan a menu in those desperate Depression years. I seldom invited company for a meal, but I did try to be prepared for unexpected Sunday dinner guests, for it was the custom in rural Colorado to drop in on neighbors for a visit. Whatever I had in the cupboard in those bartering days, when money and provisions were scarce, became part of a creative meal. When better times came along and we moved back to Iowa, one of my greatest pleasures was planning and serving a dinner or brunch for friends.

Soups and Egg Dishes

TOMATO SOUP

Elizabeth Jane

1 qt. home-canned
tomatoes, 1 can (28 oz.)
tomatoes, or 3 or 4
large fresh tomatoes,
peeled and chopped
1 small onion, chopped
1 tbsp. butter or
margarine

1 tsp. sugar
1 tsp. dried basil
½ tsp. pepper
2 cups milk
¼ tsp. soda

If using fresh garden tomatoes, remove skins by scalding with boiling water. Slip off skins, then core and cut the tomatoes. Precook the tomatoes slightly in a saucepan of water on the stove or in a covered dish in the microwave. If using canned tomatoes, either drain them or reduce milk to 1 cup.

In a saucepan, sauté the onion in butter until soft. Add remaining ingredients, mixing well. Heat thoroughly over low heat to serving temperature, but do not boil, stirring constantly. The soda helps prevent the milk from curdling. Serve with toasted croutons or crackers. Makes 4 servings.

HEARTY HAM SOUP

Vern

1 ham bone
6 cups water
4 cups raw, diced potatoes
1 onion, chopped
1 can (16 oz.) cream-style
corn

2 cups milk
¼ cup minced parsley
Salt and pepper to taste

In a large kettle, cover the ham bone with 6 cups of water. Bring to boil, then skim off foam. Cover and simmer for 2 hours. Remove bone and trim off any ham. Return meat to kettle; discard bone. Add potatoes and onion to the broth. Cover and cook until potatoes are tender, approximately 20 minutes. Stir in corn, milk, parsley, salt, and pepper. Over low heat, bring soup to a simmer, but do not boil. Serve in soup bowls with croutons on top. Makes 6 servings.

BEAN SOUP

Elizabeth

2 cups navy or great
  northern beans
1 medium onion, chopped
1 cup chopped celery
1 ham bone or 2 cups
  chopped ham
6 cups water

1 large potato, cubed
2 carrots, peeled and
  sliced
Salt to taste
¼ tsp. pepper
1 to 2 cups cream or milk

Wash and drain beans. In a large, covered kettle or dutch oven, soak beans overnight in water to cover. The next morning, drain the beans and place them in a large soup kettle with chopped onion and celery. Add the ham bone or chopped ham and 6 cups water. Bring to a boil and cook slowly, covered, for 3 hours or more, until beans are tender. Add potato, carrots, salt, and pepper. Re-cover and continue cooking until vegetables are tender, approximately 30 minutes.

If using a ham bone, remove it from the kettle. Chop meat and return meat to soup kettle; discard bone. Just before serving, add 1 or more cups of cream (preferred for a thicker, richer base) or milk to desired consistency. Heat to serving temperature, but do not boil. For a perfect meal, serve with cornbread. Makes 5 to 6 servings.

PEA SOUP
Lavina

This soup is also excellent served with cornbread.

2 cups dried split peas
1 medium onion, chopped
1 ham bone or 2 cups
  chopped ham

4 to 5 cups water
2 carrots, sliced (optional)

In a covered bowl, soak the dried peas overnight in water to cover. The next morning, drain peas and place them in a large kettle. Add the onion and ham bone or chopped ham for flavor. Pour in water. Bring to a boil, reduce heat, then cover and cook gently for at least 2 hours. After about 1 hour of cooking, add carrots. Stir often to prevent burning.

If soup gets too thick, add more water to achieve desired consistency. Makes about 4 to 6 servings.

POTATO SOUP
Jessie

Recipe tester Wynne Schafer of Davenport says that browned vegetables give this soup a nice nutty flavor.

1 medium onion, chopped
2 ribs celery, chopped
2 tbsp. butter or
  margarine
4 large raw potatoes,
  peeled and cubed (or
  precooked—baked or
  boiled)

1 cup chicken broth or
  water
2 cups milk
½ tsp. salt
¼ tsp. pepper

In a saucepan, sauté chopped onion and celery in butter until soft but not brown. Add cubed potatoes and chicken broth or water; cover and cook together over low heat until potatoes are tender, about 20 minutes for raw potatoes, less for precooked. Do not drain. Add milk, salt, and pepper, then simmer over low heat until hot. Do not boil. Serve warm. Makes about 6 servings.

Note: Leftover baked or boiled potatoes are ideal for this soup.

SALMON SOUP
Jessie

Wynne Schafer, our recipe tester in Davenport, suggested adding dried dill for taste and color. She advises not to overcook because the fish loses flavor.

3 tbsp. chopped onion
2 tbsp. butter or
  margarine
1 can (15 oz.) salmon,
  drained

1 qt. milk
Salt and pepper to taste
1 tsp. dried dill (optional)

In a saucepan, sauté chopped onions in melted butter until tender. Clean the salmon of any skin or bones, then flake and add to the onions and butter. Over low heat, stir in milk, bring to simmer, and season with salt, pepper, and dried dill. Simmer gently for 10 minutes, stirring until hot, but do not boil. Serve with oyster crackers. Makes 4 to 6 servings.

BROWN BEEF STEW
Vern

Thickened, this makes a good soup. Some cooks like to serve this over hot cooked rice or noodles. It's a good way to use leftover vegetables.

1 lb. beef stew meat,
  cubed
2 tbsp. shortening or
  vegetable oil
1 large onion, chunked
3 carrots, cut in 1-inch
  slices

2 ribs celery, chunked
Salt and pepper to taste
Dash oregano
2 potatoes, chunked
1 cup chopped tomatoes
  (optional)
2 tbsp. flour

In a saucepan, brown the meat in the fat, stirring until well browned. Add water barely to cover. Add the onion, carrots, and celery. Add seasonings as desired. Cover and cook slowly until meat and vegetables are almost tender, about 1½ hours, depending on tenderness of meat. Add the potatoes and tomatoes, cover, and cook until potatoes are tender, approximately 20 minutes. Add a small amount of water to cover if mixture cooks dry.

If thick stew is desired, mix the flour with a little cold water and stir into stew. Bring to a boil and cook until thick, stirring constantly. You may need to add water as it cooks. Makes 5 to 6 servings.

DAY LATER SOUP
Vern

After carving the meat from a turkey or chicken, use the carcass to make a delectable soup. During the Depression, we had to make use of everything, but I still use this recipe because it is so good!

1 turkey or chicken carcass	½ cup uncooked rice, white or brown
6 cups cold water	1 to 2 cups leftover
1 cup cubed carrots	vegetables (peas, corn,
1 cup chopped onion	or green beans)
1 cup chopped celery	1 cup tomato juice

In a large kettle, cover the carcass with cold water. Bring to a boil; skim off foam. Cover and cook slowly for at least 1 hour. Lift out carcass and discard the bones. Quite a bit of meat will have cooked off the bones. Leave meat in stock.

Add carrots, onion, celery, rice, and leftover vegetables to the stock. Cover and cook slowly for about 30 minutes, or until rice is done, adding tomato juice as needed. Heat to serving temperature. Makes 6 servings.

HOW TO TELL GOOD EGGS
Sara

Put eggs in water. If the large end turns up, they are not fresh. This is a rule that will not fail.

FRIED EGGS
Elizabeth

Fresh eggs (enough to feed your family)	Vinegar (optional)
Fresh butter or vegetable oil	

Fried eggs are a popular dish. Fresh butter, hissing in the pan, warns the family that dinner soon will be served. Break each egg and slip it into the pan. One minute or two and all the noise is over. Sprinkled with pepper and salt and a few drops of vinegar, the eggs are ready to be served.

With fried potatoes and onions, sausage or ham, pancakes, and toast, this makes an evening meal.

HOW TO MAKE BUTTER
Elizabeth Jane

**Fresh cream, separated
from fresh milk**

**Cold water
1 tbsp. fine salt**

Start with cream from one cow's milk. To separate the cream from the milk, use fresh milk from the cow and strain it into clean pans. Set it over low heat until scalded, but do not let it boil. When it is cooled, skim off the cream. The milk will still be fit for ordinary use.

When you have accumulated enough cream, put it in an earthen basin, and beat it with a spoon until butter forms. Remove it from any remaining milk and work in a little cold water. Put a tablespoon of fine salt in each pound of butter. Form into a roll and wrap in clean muslin. This makes a welcomed Christmas gift or gift for any occasion.

BAKED EGGS
Jessie

**Butter or nonstick
 vegetable cooking spray
12 strips bacon
12 eggs
Salt and pepper to taste**

**12 tbsp. cream
6 tsp. grated American
 cheese or 12 small
 strips of American
 cheese (optional)**

Butter 12 muffin cups, or spray with a nonstick vegetable cooking spray. Heat oven to 350 degrees.

In a skillet, fry bacon slightly, but do not overcook. Ring each muffin cup with a strip of bacon. Break 1 egg into each muffin cup. Add salt and pepper to taste, then put 1 tablespoon of cream on top of each egg and sprinkle ½ teaspoon grated cheese on each, if desired.

Bake at 350 degrees for about 20 minutes, until the eggs are cooked as your family prefers them. Makes 12 servings.

CREAMED EGGS ON TOAST
Vern

I learned how to make this dish in cooking class in the seventh grade—more than seventy-five years ago. When I was a bride, it served me well.

6 eggs
3 tbsp. butter
3 tbsp. flour

¼ tsp. salt
2 cups milk
3 slices toast

Hard-cook eggs, cool, then peel and separate the whites and yolks. Chop the whites only. Reserve the egg yolks. Make a white sauce by melting butter in a skillet or saucepan over low heat, then adding flour and salt. Stir over low heat until the mixture is smooth and bubbly. Slowly add milk, stirring constantly and cooking until thick. Remove from heat and stir in chopped egg whites. Pour over 3 slices of toast. Rub the egg yolks through a sieve and sprinkle on top. Makes 3 servings.

SOUR CREAM QUICHE
Vern

This quiche is different and rich. For variety, substitute 1 cup of diced ham for the bacon.

1 unbaked 9-inch pie shell
8 slices bacon, fried crisp
  and crumbled
1½ cups shredded
  cheddar cheese
4 eggs

1 cup sour cream
¼ cup half-and-half
1 tbsp. flour
½ tsp. salt
¼ tsp. pepper

Heat oven to 375 degrees. Sprinkle meat and cheese over the bottom of the pie shell.

In a mixing bowl, combine eggs, sour cream, half-and-half, flour, salt, and pepper; mix well. Carefully pour egg and sour cream mixture into pie shell. Bake at 375 degrees for 20 to 25 minutes, until lightly browned. Let set for 5 to 10 minutes before cutting and serving. Makes 6 servings.

BREAKFAST OR BRUNCH EGG CASSEROLE
Vern

Prepare this casserole a day ahead or time and refrigerate overnight.

6 slices bread, crusts removed	**2 cups milk**
2 cups grated cheddar cheese	**½ tsp. dry mustard**
	½ tsp. salt
4 eggs, lightly beaten	**4 slices bacon, fried crisp and crumbled**

Butter an 8 x 8-inch baking dish. Cut the bread in cubes. Alternate layers of bread and grated cheese in prepared dish. In a mixing bowl, combine eggs, milk, mustard and salt; mix well. Pour milk mixture over the bread and cheese. Cover and refrigerate overnight.

The next morning, remove dish from refrigerator and uncover. Heat oven to 350 degrees. Bake, uncovered, for 1 hour. When done, sprinkle with hot crumbled bacon and serve. Serves 4 to 6 generously.

Note: If bacon is fried ahead of time and refrigerated, it should be warmed in the microwave, or it may added to the casserole 10 to 15 minutes before removing from the oven. Double the recipe for a 9 x 13 x 2-inch dish.

PARTY SCRAMBLED EGGS
WITH CHEESE SAUCE
Vern

This is great for brunch or breakfast; I won a prize with this recipe in a contest sponsored by the Quad-City Times *in Davenport Iowa.*

EGGS:

Nonstick vegetable
  cooking spray
¼ cup chopped green
  onions
6 tbsp. butter
1 cup diced, cooked
  Canadian bacon or ham

12 eggs, slightly beaten
1 can (3 oz.) mushroom
  pieces, drained
¾ cup cracker crumbs or
  bread crumbs

CHEESE SAUCE:

2 tbsp. butter
2 tbsp. flour
2 cups milk
½ tsp. salt

¼ tsp. pepper
1 cup shredded American
  cheese

Prepare cheese sauce. Melt butter in a large saucepan over low heat. Blend in flour until mixture is smooth. Add milk, stirring and cooking over low heat until mixture thickens and is creamy. Add cheese and blend until melted. Set aside.

Lightly grease a 9 x 13 x 2-inch pan or baking dish with nonstick vegetable cooking spray. Heat oven to 350 degrees. In a large skillet, sauté onions in 3 tablespoons butter until tender, then add the meat. Add eggs and scramble, but keep them slightly moist. Fold egg mixture and mushrooms into the cheese sauce. Pour into prepared baking dish.

Melt remaining 3 tablespoons butter or margarine in a frying pan or a microwave dish and stir in bread or cracker crumbs until moistened. Sprinkle on the casserole. Bake at 350 degrees for 30 minutes. Makes 6 servings.

EGGS IN SHRIMP SAUCE

Vern

EGGS:

9 hard-cooked eggs,
  peeled
½ cup mayonnaise
½ tsp. salt
½ tsp. paprika

¼ tsp. mustard
½ tsp. curry powder
  (optional)
Fresh parsley

SHRIMP SAUCE:

2 tbsp. butter
4 tsp. flour
1 can (10¾ oz.) cream of
  shrimp soup

1 soup can filled with milk
½ cup shredded sharp
  cheddar cheese
1 cup bread crumbs

To prepare shrimp sauce, melt the butter in a saucepan, over low heat. Stir in flour and cook, stirring over low heat until smooth. Slowly stir in the soup and milk, cooking and stirring until sauce thickens and is creamy. Add cheese and stir until melted. Set aside.

Heat oven to 350 degrees. Butter a 1-quart casserole. Cut eggs in half lengthwise. Remove yolks and mash. Mix the yolks with mayonnaise and seasonings. Fill the egg white halves with egg yolk mixture. Arrange in prepared casserole dish. Cover with shrimp sauce. Bake at 350 degrees for 20 minutes. Garnish with fresh parsley. Makes 9 servings.

Frustrated Gourmet

I like to bake a loaf of bread
But he likes baker's bread instead.
Creative cooking, spices rare,
He likes his chicken better bare.

Meringues and pastries, cakes so high,
He still prefers just apple pie.
Then comes the day when cooking bores
When writing verses call . . .

And I'm glad for soup in cans,
He doesn't mind at all.

Breads, Rolls, Muffins, and Coffee Cakes

SHORTBREAD
Elizabeth

This shortbread recipe is from the mid-1800s. It is very rich and is baked as one piece. When served, each person breaks off a portion. Home economist and recipe tester Bonnie Moeller, of Bettendorf, rated shortbread excellent and commented that it tasted every bit as scrumptious as the real Scottish shortbread in Edinburgh. It must be made with real butter for this wonderful taste.

1 cup granulated sugar
4 cups flour

2 cups butter (at room temperature)

In a large mixing bowl, combine sugar and 3 cups flour; mix well. Cut in butter until mixture is crumbly. Add more flour if needed to make a very stiff dough. Knead on a lightly floured board for about 20 minutes. Roll out like a pie pastry and place the whole piece of dough in an ungreased jelly-roll pan. Bake at 300 degrees for 30 to 35 minutes. Makes 10 to 12 servings.

JOHNNY CAKE
Sara

This was also called Journey Cake because it could be made with water and it traveled well. The recipe calls for sweet milk as opposed to the sour milk, which was often used by cooks in the early days.

1 egg
2 cups stone-ground cornmeal

1 tsp. salt
1½ cups sweet milk or water

Beat the egg in a medium-size bowl. Stir in cornmeal and salt. Add milk or water; mix well. Drop batter by spoonfuls onto a hot griddle and fry until brown on both sides. Makes 12 Johnny cakes.

Note: Gradually, through the years, other ingredients were added to Johnny Cake as they became available. Another version calls for 1 cup of sweet milk, 1 cup buttermilk, 1 teaspoon salt, and 1 tablespoon shortening. Spread the mixture ½ inch thick on a buttered tin or shallow pan, then bake. As soon as the cake begins to brown, baste it with a rag tied to a stick and dipped in melted butter. Repeat five or six times until brown and crispy. Break apart before serving.

SOUTHERN-STYLE SPOON BREAD
Sara

Spoon Bread is dished out of the bowl in which it is prepared with a spoon. It is not cut or sliced like a loaf of bread. This recipe is large, obviously for a family of twelve or a barn-raising or harvesting crew according to tester Bonnie Moeller.

1 qt. whole milk	**¼ lb. butter or bacon fat,**
Pinch salt	**melted**
1¼ cups cornmeal (white	**8 eggs**
preferred)	

In a saucepan, combine milk and salt, and warm over low heat to remove the chill. Slowly stir in cornmeal until mixture is smooth. Remove from heat and add melted butter or bacon fat and 4 of the eggs. Beat well. Return to a low heat and beat in remaining 4 eggs, one at a time until well blended. Do not boil.

Heat oven to 350 degrees. Pour batter into a buttered 2-quart bowl or casserole dish, and bake until knife inserted in center comes out clean, about 1 hour. Makes 1 loaf.

BERRY TEA CAKES
Elizabeth Jane

Bonnie Moeller tested this recipe with blueberries. She noted, "These are more of a muffin than a cake. There is very little sugar in them. This, however, was probably typical of recipes from the late 1800s—not much sugar."

3 tbsp. butter
2 tbsp. sugar
1 egg
1 tsp. cream of tartar
½ tsp. baking soda
1 cup sweet milk

2 cups flour
1 cup fruit (peeled and diced apples, pitted cherries, or wild berries in season)

In a mixing bowl, cream butter and sugar thoroughly. Beat in egg. In a small bowl, stir cream of tartar and baking soda into milk. Mix well, then add to creamed mixture. Sift flour and add gradually to milk mixture to make a stiff batter. Stir in fruit.

Heat oven to 425 degrees. Pour batter into greased muffin tins. Bake for 15 to 20 minutes. These are to be eaten with butter. Makes 12 muffins.

FRIED CORNMEAL MUSH
Elizabeth Jane

Mixing the cornmeal first with 1 cup cold water and then adding it to the boiling water keeps the cornmeal from lumping.

4 cups water
1 cup yellow or white cornmeal

1 tsp. salt
3 tbsp. shortening, melted

Mix cornmeal with 1 cup of cold water. Put remaining 3 cups of water into a clean dinner pot or stew pan, cover it, and bring it to a boil. Add salt. Remove the light scum that appears on top. Slowly add cornmeal mixture, stirring constantly with a pudding stick (wooden spoon) until thickened. Stir in melted shortening. Stir a while longer; simmer about 5 to 10 minutes. Makes 6 to 8 servings.

Note: As a side dish for a meal, pour into a dish and serve hot with milk or butter, syrup or sugar, or with meat and gravy, the same as potatoes or rice. Pour leftovers into 9 x 5 x 3-inch bread pans, and refrigerate for frying. The cornmeal mush needs to cool to set up for slicing and frying later. To prepare, cut mush into pieces 1 inch thick and 3 inches long. Dip each piece in well-beaten egg, roll in cracker crumbs or flour, and fry in butter or margarine. Serve hot.

BAKING POWDER BISCUITS
Lavina

Grandma made biscuits almost every morning.

2 cups flour	**½ tsp. salt**
4 tsp. baking powder	**½ cup shortening**
2 tsp. sugar	**About 1 cup milk**

In a medium-size bowl, mix flour, baking powder, sugar and salt. Cut in shortening. Make a well and pour in milk. Stir until doughy. Turn out onto a lightly floured board. Knead 4 times and roll out dough to ½ inch thick. Cut with a biscuit cutter.

Heat oven to 400 degrees. Bake biscuits on an ungreased cookie sheet for about 10 minutes. Makes 15 to 20 biscuits.

DOUGHNUTS
Lavina

Early cooks gave no directions for frying. Housewives had to be experienced or depend on Mom for advice!

3 eggs	4 cups sifted flour
1 cup sugar	3 tsp. baking powder
4 tbsp. lard, melted	½ tsp. salt
1 capful vanilla (1 tsp.)	¼ tsp. nutmeg
1 cup milk	Oil (for deep frying)

In a medium-size bowl, beat eggs well. Beat in sugar, melted lard, and vanilla. Stir in milk. In a smaller bowl, combine flour, baking powder, salt, and nutmeg; then blend into egg mixture, beating until smooth. Turn out onto a generously floured bread board and cover both sides of dough lightly with flour. Roll out gently until ⅓ inch thick. Using a floured doughnut cutter, cut doughnuts and save the holes.

Pour oil 3 to 4 inches deep in a skillet or deep fryer, and heat to 365 degrees, or until a cube of bread browns in about 60 seconds. Lift each doughnut or hole with a spatula and gently drop it into the hot oil. Fry only as many at one time as can be turned easily. When doughnuts float on top, turn and continue cooking until a golden brown, about 3 minutes. Remove from hot oil with a long fork, and drain on paper toweling spread over newspapers.

Serve doughnuts plain, dipped in powdered sugar, glazed in assorted flavors—chocolate, cherry, or vanilla. Or, gently shake doughnuts in a bag of powdered sugar. Makes about 3 dozen doughnuts and 3 dozen doughnut holes.

DUMPLINGS
Lavina

Grandma Lavina's dumplings were always light and fluffy.

1 egg
²⁄₃ cup light cream
1 cup flour

1 heaping tsp. baking
   powder
Chicken broth (for boiling)

In a cup, beat egg into light cream. In a mixing bowl, combine flour and baking powder. Add cream-egg mixture to flour; mix well.

After stewing a chicken, remove chicken from kettle and reserve broth. Bring broth to boil. Drop dumpling batter by tablespoonful into gently boiling chicken broth. Each should sink, then float and turn over, or they may be turned with a spoon. Cover and cook for about 12 to 15 minutes. Makes 8 to 10 dumplings.

PARKER HOUSE ROLLS
Jessie

A recipe of Jessie's era took more time than today's recipes. This one has three risings.

2 pkg. active dry yeast
1 cup warm water
4 to 4½ cups flour
¼ cup sugar

½ cup shortening
3 large eggs, beaten
1 tsp. salt
2 tbsp. butter, softened

In a large bowl, dissolve yeast in warm water. Stir in flour with a spoon. In another large bowl, cream together sugar and shortening. Add beaten eggs, salt, and then flour-yeast mixture; mix well. Cover and let rise in a warm place for about 1½ hours, or until doubled in size.

Punch dough down, cover, and let rise again until it falls in middle; stir down with a spoon. Spoon onto a lightly floured board and roll into a rectangle. Cut and shape into dinner rolls—Parker House or any desired shape. Use only enough flour on the board to keep the dough from being sticky.

Make Parker House rolls by making small balls and flattening the balls into round circles in your hand (or use a cookie cutter). Lightly grease rolls with oil or butter, and fold them in half. Place on a greased cookie sheet about an inch apart. These need to rise again until double in size, which takes 45 minutes to an hour.

Toward the end of the last rising time, heat oven to 350 degrees. Bake for about 15 minutes, until nicely browned. Do not overbake. Makes 2 to 3 dozen Parker House rolls, depending on size. Smaller is better.

Note: To make cinnamon rolls, roll out a sheet of dough, spread with butter, sprinkle with sugar and cinnamon, roll up along the long side, and cut into 1-inch slices. Place cut side down in a greased 9 x 13-inch pan. Cover and let rise until doubled in bulk. Bake at 350 degrees for 20 minutes. Makes 2 dozen rolls.

CORN FRITTERS
Jessie

This is one way to use leftover corn, and it shows how earlier cooks varied their menus. Today's cooks would use whole kernel corn for this recipe.

2 eggs, separated	**1¼ cups flour**
1 cup milk	**1 tsp. baking powder**
½ tsp. salt (or less)	**Shortening or vegetable oil**
¼ tsp. pepper	**(for frying)**
1 cup cold chopped corn	

Separate yolks from whites of two eggs. Set whites aside. In a medium-size bowl, beat yolks until thick and lemon-colored. Add milk, salt, pepper, corn, flour, and baking powder. Beat egg whites to a stiff froth and fold them into the batter. Drop from a tablespoon into hot lard (oil) in skillet or frypan, and fry to a delicate brown. Makes 12 to 15 fritters.

SOUR CREAM CAKES
OR COOKY BUNS
Jessie

Mom's specialty! I found this recipe in the attic after my mother passed away in 1950. I changed the name, reduced the amount of sugar, entered it in the Fifth Pillsbury Bake-Off, and won a trip to New York, where I made it for the Grand National Contest. In addition to my first trip to New York, my prizes included an electric stove, a mixer, and $100!

1 pkg. active dry yeast or ⅝ oz. cake compressed yeast
¼ cup warm water
3 cups flour
1 tsp. salt
½ cup shortening
⅓ cup sugar
1 tsp. grated lemon rind
1 tbsp. lemon juice
5 eggs, separated (reserve whites)
¾ cup sour cream
Sugar (for sprinkling)

In a small bowl, dissolve yeast in warm water. In another bowl, sift flour with salt. In a larger bowl, cream together shortening, ⅓ cup sugar, grated lemon rind, and lemon juice. Add unbeaten egg yolks, sour cream, and yeast-water mixture. Gradually blend in dry ingredients. Beat well. Do not let rise. Drop by teaspoonful onto greased baking sheets. Cover and let stand in a warm place until doubled in size, 30 to 60 minutes.

Heat oven to 350 degrees. Slightly beat reserved egg whites. Brush buns with egg whites and sprinkle buns generously with sugar. Bake at 350 degrees for about 15 to 20 minutes, until golden brown. Serve warm. Yields 3 dozen.

Note: Dough may be covered and stored in refrigerator for up to five days and baked as needed.

COMPANY FRENCH TOAST
Vern

This recipe is unusual and easy. Most of the work is done ahead of serving time.

8 slices French bread, cut
  ¾ inch thick
4 eggs
1 cup milk
2 tbsp. orange juice
1 tbsp. sugar

½ tsp. vanilla
¼ tsp. salt (or less)
¼ cup butter or margarine
  (for frying)
Confectioners' sugar
Syrup or jelly

Arrange bread in a single layer in a large baking dish. In a mixing bowl, beat eggs and milk together. Add orange juice, sugar, vanilla, and salt. Pour over the bread. Turn the slices to coat well. Cover and refrigerate overnight.

The next morning, gently fry slices of bread on both sides in hot butter until browned. Sprinkle with confectioners' sugar. Serve with syrup or jelly, if preferred. Serves 4.

CLOTHES PIN SPINS
Vern

This is a versatile recipe that's fun to use. Clothes Pin Spins are ideal for a tea or afternoon coffee. I often use the coffee cake variation; it freezes well.

1 pkg. dry yeast
1 cup milk, scalded and
  cooled
4 cups flour
1 tsp. salt
3 tbsp. sugar
1 cup vegetable shortening
  or margarine

2 eggs, lightly beaten
Melted butter (for
  brushing)
1 egg white, lightly beaten
1 tbsp. water
Granulated sugar
Jelly

In a small bowl, soften yeast in lukewarm milk. Mix flour, salt, and 3 tablespoons sugar in a large bowl. Cut in the shortening as if you were making pie dough. Add beaten eggs and milk-yeast mixture. Stir all together with a spoon. Do not knead. Dough will be very soft. Cover and refrigerate for at least 2 hours or overnight. (It will keep in the refrigerator for a week.)

When preparing to bake, grease 2 or 3 cookie sheets, depending on size. On a lightly floured board, roll out dough in 3 portions, as thick as pie dough, each in an oblong shape. Brush each with melted butter, then cut into strips 1 inch wide. Wrap each strip around a well-greased round clothes pin, the buttered side next to the pin. Place on greased cookie sheets without allowing rolls to touch. Cover and let rise for 1 hour, or until doubled.

Heat oven to 350 degrees. Lightly beat egg white, and mix with 1 tablespoon water. Brush tops of spins. Sprinkle with granulated sugar. Bake at 350 degrees for 12 to 15 minutes, or until browned. When done, remove clothes pins at once, and cool spins on racks. Fill each spin with jelly. Makes 3 dozen spins.

COFFEE CAKE VARIATION
FOR CLOTHES PIN SPINS
Vern

1 recipe Clothes Pin Spins dough (see recipe above)	**1½ cup chopped nuts (optional)**
6 tbsp. butter	**3 cups fruit (apples,**
6 tsp. cinnamon	**cranberries, dates, or**
1 cup sugar	**commercial pie filling)**

Grease 3 pie tins. After mixing, cover and place dough in refrigerator and chill for at least 2 hours or overnight. Once dough has been chilled, roll out on lightly floured board in 3 large circles. Spread each circle with 2 tablespoons butter, then sprinkle each with 2 teaspoons cinnamon, ⅓ cup sugar, and ½ cup nuts. Spread 1 cup fruit filling on each circle. Any fruit filling may be used, such as apples, cranberries, or dates.

Heat oven to 350 degrees. Roll up each circle in jelly-roll fashion; take one end of the roll and tuck it inside the other end, forming a ring. Place each ring, cut side down, in a well-greased pie tin. Cover and let rise for about 2 hours, until doubled in size. The dough may be slashed so it can expand, but this step is not necessary. Bake at 350 degrees for 20 to 25 minutes. Cool on racks. Frost and decorate, as desired. Makes 3 coffee cakes.

BREAD STICKS
Vern

This recipe is simple to make, crunchy, and has a nice color. Our tester, Bonnie Moeller of Bettendorf, says that you really need to watch it closely because it browns quickly.

1 pkg. active dry yeast
²/₃ cup warm water
2 cups flour
1 tbsp. sugar
¼ cup soft shortening
1 egg, beaten

1 tbsp. water
1 tsp. salt (kosher or coarse)
Sesame seeds or poppy seeds

In a small bowl, dissolve yeast in warm water. In a medium-size bowl, combine 1 cup of flour, sugar, and shortening; mix well. Add yeast-water mixture and remaining cup of flour. Turn dough out onto a lightly floured board and knead until smooth and elastic. Cover and let rise in a warm place until doubled in bulk. Punch dough down and cut into 48 pieces. Roll each piece to 8 inches in length.

Heat oven to 400 degrees. Place bread sticks ½ inch apart on 2 greased baking sheets. In a measuring cup or small bowl, beat egg with 1 tablespoon water. Brush over bread sticks. Sprinkle with coarse salt and sesame seeds or poppy seeds. If soft, puffy breadsticks are desired, let rise until doubled in size, about 30 minutes, but this is not necessary. Bake at 400 degrees for 20 minutes. Watch closely. Makes 48 bread sticks.

ALL-PURPOSE BUNS
Vern

These can be made into dinner rolls, cinnamon rolls, or whatever other baked goods that you choose.

⅔ cup milk
⅔ cup sugar
1 tsp. salt
⅓ cup margarine
2 pkg. active dry yeast
⅔ cup warm water

3 eggs, well-beaten
½ tsp. nutmeg
5¾ cups flour
Egg wash (1 egg beaten
   with 2 tbsp. water)

In a medium-size saucepan, scald milk. Remove from heat; stir in sugar, salt, and margarine. Cool to lukewarm. In a small bowl, sprinkle yeast into warm water and stir to dissolve. Add 3 beaten eggs and nutmeg.

In a large bowl, combine milk and yeast mixtures. Add 3 cups of flour and beat until smooth. Turn out onto a floured board, gradually adding about 2¾ cups more flour, keeping the dough very soft. Knead for 10 minutes.

Place dough in a large, greased bowl to rise. Oil the top with butter, and cover with a damp cloth. Let rise for 1 hour. Punch dough down and turn over. Let rest for 10 minutes. Turn the dough out onto a lightly floured board and cut into 24 parts. Roll each part into a ball and place balls on 2 greased cookie sheets. Brush each ball with egg wash. Cover and let rise for 1 hour.

Heat oven to 400 degrees. Bake for 20 minutes, or until browned. Makes 24 rolls. Dough may be used for other shapes as well.

POTATO DINNER ROLLS
Vern

1 pkg. dry yeast
½ cup lukewarm water
⅔ cup shortening
½ cup sugar
1 cup prepared mashed
   potatoes

1 cup scalded milk, cooled
   to lukewarm
2 eggs, beaten
6½ cups flour, divided
1 tsp. salt

In a small bowl or cup, soften yeast in warm water. In a large mixing bowl, cream shortening and sugar until fluffy. Add yeast mixture. Mix in mashed potatoes, milk, eggs, 2 cups flour, and salt. Using a spoon, stir in enough additional flour to make a soft dough. Cover and let rise in a warm place for 1 hour.

Turn dough out onto a floured board, using enough flour to be able to handle the dough. Kneading is not necessary. Grease 2 or 3 baking sheets. Heat oven to 400 degrees.

Form dough into any shape—cloverleaf, Parker House, or crescent rolls. Place cloverleaf rolls in greased muffin tins and other shapes on greased baking sheets. Cover and let rise until doubled in size, about 30 minutes. Bake at 400 degrees for about 20 minutes. Serve hot. Makes about 3 dozen rolls.

OLD-TIME CINNAMON ROLLS
Vern

Another contest winner!

2 pkg. dry yeast
½ cup lukewarm water
¼ cup sugar
⅓ cup shortening
1 tsp. salt
1 cup milk

3 eggs
4 to 5 cups flour
¼ cup butter
1 cup brown sugar
1 to 2 tsp. cinnamon

In a small bowl, soften yeast in warm water. In another small bowl, cream sugar, shortening, and salt together. In a saucepan, scald milk, then cool to lukewarm. In a large mixing bowl, beat eggs and add milk and yeast mixture. Add creamed mixture along with enough flour to make the dough as stiff as possible when mixing with a spoon. Do not handle (knead). Cover with a damp cloth. Let rise for 1 hour.

Dough will be sticky. Using a spoon, scrape out onto a well-floured board. Spread dough out, and pat with flour until rolled very thin. Spread with about ¼ cup butter. Sprinkle generously with brown sugar and cinnamon. Roll up jelly-roll fashion. Cut in slices about 1 inch thick. Place cut side down and line rolls side by side in a well-greased 9 x 13 x 2-inch pan. Let rise until doubled in size.

Heat oven to 350 degrees. Bake for about 25 minutes, or until browned. Remove from the oven and turn out onto a towel or cooling rack, or the caramel filling will stick to the pan as it cools. Transfer to a platter. Frost with a glaze or serve plain, but they are best served warm. They may be reheated before serving. Makes about 20 rolls.

CRISPY VIENNA ROLLS
Vern

My father, a professional baker, gave me the tip of baking rolls in steam.

1 pkg. dry yeast	2 tbsp. margarine
4 cups flour	3 egg whites
1 tbsp. sugar	1 tbsp. water
1 tsp. salt	Poppy seeds or sesame
1 cup water	seeds (optional)

In a large bowl, thoroughly mix dry yeast with flour, sugar, and salt. In a small saucepan, heat water; add margarine and mix well. Let cool to lukewarm.

In the large bowl of an electric mixer, combine lukewarm water and 1⅓ cups of the flour mixture. Beat for 2 minutes. In the small bowl of the electric mixer, beat 2 egg whites until stiff peaks form. Add beaten egg whites and remaining flour mixture to dough. Turn out onto a floured board and knead until smooth and springy, at least 5 minutes. Put dough in a large greased bowl. Turn dough to grease top. Cover and let rise until doubled, about 1½ hours. Return dough to same board, divide into rolls and place them on 2 greased baking sheets.

In a small bowl, slightly beat remaining egg white with 1 tbsp. water. Brush some of the egg white mixture on the rolls. Sprinkle with poppy or sesame seeds, if desired. On the baking sheets, cover and let rolls rise until doubled in size, then brush again with egg white and water mixture.

Heat oven to 400 degrees. Fill a flat pan, such as a jelly-roll pan, with boiling water and place in the bottom of the oven. Place sheets of rolls on middle rack in oven. The steam baking makes the rolls hard and crisp, like bakery hard rolls. Bake at 400 degrees for 15 to 20 minutes.

When the rolls are half done, I sometimes brush them again with the egg-white mixture. Makes about 20 to 24 rolls.

ORANGE ROLLS
Vern

1 pkg. dry yeast
¼ cup warm water
½ cup vegetable shortening
⅓ cup sugar
1 tsp. salt

1 cup milk, scalded
2 eggs, beaten
¼ cup orange juice
2 tbsp. grated orange rind
5 cups flour

In a small saucepan, dissolve yeast in warm water. In a large bowl, measure shortening, sugar, and salt. Pour scalded, hot milk over shortening mixture. Cool. Add eggs, orange juice, orange rind, and yeast mixture. Add flour a little at a time, beating thoroughly until a soft dough is obtained. Do not knead. Scrape dough into a greased bowl, turn to grease top, cover, and let rise until light, about 1 hour.

Section off for rolls; shape as desired. Place rolls on 3 or 4 greased baking sheets, about a dozen to a sheet; cover and let rise again until doubled. Heat oven to 350 degrees. Bake for 15 to 20 minutes, until golden brown. Makes 3½ to 4 dozen rolls.

Note: Drizzle a frosting glaze over the rolls while hot, if desired. See index for Confectioners' Sugar Glaze recipe.

ORANGE KISS ME ROLLS
Vern

1 pkg. dry yeast	½ cup sour cream
¼ cup warm water	3½ cups flour
1 cup sugar, divided	½ cup butter, melted
1 tsp. salt	2 tbsp. grated orange rind
2 eggs, beaten	

GLAZE:

¼ cup butter	2 tbsp. frozen orange juice
¾ cup sugar	concentrate
½ cup sour cream	

In a large bowl, dissolve yeast in warm water. Beat in ¼ cup sugar, salt, eggs, and sour cream. Add 2 cups of flour, and beat well. Add 6 tablespoons of the melted butter, and stir in the remainder of the flour to make a soft dough. Turn out onto a lightly floured board and knead until dough is smooth and elastic, adding additional flour if needed. Place in a greased bowl, turn to grease top, cover, and let rise in a warm place for 2 hours. This rich dough needs the additional rising time.

On a floured board, punch dough down and knead about 15 times. Divide dough in half, then roll each piece into a 13-inch circle. Brush with remaining 2 tablespoons of butter. Combine remaining ¾ cup sugar and orange rind and sprinkle half of mixture on each circle. Cut each circle into 12 wedges. Roll up like crescents. Place crescents on 2 greased cookie sheets. Cover and let rise until doubled, about 1 hour.

Heat oven to 350 degrees. Bake for 12 minutes. While hot, make glaze. Mix glaze ingredients together in a saucepan and boil for 3 minutes. Brush glaze on rolls while they still are hot. Makes 24 rolls.

APRICOT NUT BREAD
Vern

For the holidays, substitute 1 cup candied cherries and ½ cup mixed fruits for the apricots.

1½ cups fresh apricots, washed, pitted, and dried
2 tbsp. butter
½ cup sugar
1 egg, well beaten

1¼ cups milk
2½ cups flour
3 tsp. baking powder
½ tsp. salt
1 cup nuts, chopped

Put apricots through a grinder or food processor. In a mixing bowl, cream butter and sugar. Add egg and milk. In a medium-size bowl, sift together the dry ingredients and add to creamed mixture. Mix well, but do not beat. Stir in apricots and nuts.

Heat oven to 350 degrees. Grease a 9 x 5 x 3-inch loaf pan. Place dough in prepared pan. Bake for 1 hour. Remove from pan and cool before cutting. Makes 1 loaf.

BUTTER AND EGG BRAN BREAD
Vern

This recipe came from my sister's mother-in-law and has been enjoyed by my family for more than forty years. It is a very different bran bread—light in color and sweeter than most breads—and delicious when toasted. It is a must at our family Christmas celebrations, and it makes a great gift for friends.

1 cup bran cereal	¾ cup sugar
1½ tsp. salt	⅓ cup butter or
2 pkg. dry yeast	margarine, softened
1 cup lukewarm water	2 eggs
1 cup boiling water	5½ cups flour

In a large bowl, measure bran cereal and salt. In a cup or small bowl, dissolve yeast in 1 cup lukewarm water. Pour boiling water over bran and salt. Add sugar and butter or margarine; mix well. Cool to lukewarm. Stir in yeast mixture and eggs. Add 3 cups flour and beat well. Add remaining flour. Turn out onto a lightly floured board and knead until light and elastic, 6 to 8 minutes. Place dough in a large, greased bowl, turning to grease top. Cover and let rise until doubled.

Grease 2 large pans, 9 x 5½ x 3 inches, or 3 small loaf pans, 7½ x 3 x 2½ inches. Form dough into 2 large or 3 small loaves and place in prepared pans. Cover and let rise until doubled.

Heat oven to 350 degrees. Bake for 45 to 50 minutes for large loaves, 45 minutes for smaller loaves. Remove from pans. Brush with oil or butter. Cool on racks. Makes 2 large or 3 small loaves.

CANNED BREAD
Vern

This bread is baked in small coffee cans!

1 pkg. dry yeast
½ cup warm water
1 can (5.33 oz.)
  evaporated milk
3 tbsp. vegetable oil

3 tbsp. sugar
1 tsp. salt
1 cup whole wheat flour
3 cups white flour

Generously grease two 1-pound coffee cans. In a large bowl, soften yeast in warm water. Add evaporated milk, oil, sugar, and salt. In a medium-size bowl, mix flours together and add gradually to yeast mixture. Do not knead. Divide batter between the 2 greased coffee cans. Place the plastic caps on cans. Let dough rise for about 1½ hours, until caps are forced off.

Heat oven to 400 degrees. Place cans in an upright position on the oven shelf. Bake for 30 to 40 minutes, or until tops are browned. Remove bread from the cans before cooling; cool on racks. Makes 2 loaves.

CHEESE BREAD
Vern

1 cup milk
3 tbsp. sugar
1 tbsp. salt
1 tbsp. shortening
2 pkg. dry yeast

1 cup warm water
1 cup cheddar cheese,
  grated
4½ cups flour

In a medium-size saucepan, scald milk. Stir in sugar, salt, and shortening. Let stand until lukewarm.

In a cup or small bowl, dissolve yeast in warm water. Transfer to large bowl and add milk mixture and cheese. Gradually stir in flour, blending well. Do not knead. Cover and let rise until doubled in bulk.

Grease two 9 x 5 x 3-inch loaf pans. Stir or punch down the batter. Beat for half a minute. Turn into bread pans. Cover and let rise for about 1 hour. Heat oven to 375 degrees. Bake for 1 hour. Remove bread from pans and cool on a rack. Serve warm. Makes 2 loaves.

FRUIT BREAD
Vern

¼ cup butter or margarine
1 cup sugar
2 eggs
2 cups flour
1 tsp. baking soda
1 cup ripe, mashed
   bananas

¼ cup drained and
   chopped maraschino
   cherries
¼ cup chocolate chips
¼ cup chopped walnuts

Heat oven to 350 degrees. Grease a 9 x 5 x 3-inch loaf pan. In a large mixing bowl, cream butter and sugar. Add eggs, and beat well. In another bowl, sift flour and soda, then add alternately with the mashed bananas to the creamed mixture. Mix in maraschino cherries, chocolate chips, and chopped nuts. Pour into prepared loaf pan. Bake at 350 degrees for 1 hour. Cool for a short time before removing from pan. Makes 1 loaf.

Note: A thin, powdered sugar glaze may be added when loaf is removed from the oven. See index for Confectioners' Sugar Glaze recipe.

GRAPENUTS BREAD
Vern

2 cups milk
2 tbsp. vinegar
1 cup Grapenuts cereal
2 cups sugar
4 tbsp. butter or
   margarine, melted

2 eggs
4 cups flour
2 tsp. salt
1½ tsp. baking soda
2 tsp. baking powder

Heat oven to 350 degrees. Grease two 9 x 5 x 3-inch loaf pans. In a large bowl, make sour milk by adding vinegar to milk. Let stand for a few minutes until mixture thickens slightly.

Soak cereal in sour milk for 30 minutes. Add sugar, butter or margarine, and eggs. Beat until smooth, and stir in dry ingredients. Pour into greased loaf pans. Bake at 350 degrees for 50 to 60 minutes. Remove from pans at once, and cool on racks before slicing. Makes 2 loaves.

QUICK APPLE BREAD
Vern

This is a nice, moist bread with a tangy orange flavor.

½ cup shortening
1 cup sugar
1 tsp. vanilla
2 eggs
2 cups flour
¼ tsp. salt
1 tsp. baking soda

1 tsp. baking powder
2 tbsp. sour milk or
  buttermilk
1 cup finely chopped
  apples
¼ cup chopped nuts
1 tbsp. grated orange rind

Grease a 9 x 5 x 3-inch loaf pan. Heat oven to 350 degrees. In a large bowl, cream shortening, sugar, and vanilla until light and fluffy. Add eggs and beat well. In another bowl, sift together flour, salt, baking soda, and baking powder. Add flour mixture to creamed mixture alternately with milk and apples. Stir in nuts and orange rind. Pour batter into prepared pan. Bake at 350 degrees for 1 hour. Cool. Remove from the pan immediately. Makes 1 loaf.

OATMEAL BREAD
Vern

2 pkg. dry yeast
¼ cup warm water
1 cup plus 4 tbsp. regular
  or quick-cooking oats
1 tbsp. salt
⅓ cup shortening

½ cup molasses
1¼ cups boiling water
4 cups white flour
2 eggs, beaten
Egg wash (1 egg mixed
  with 1 tbsp. water)

Grease 2 loaf pans, 8½ x 4½ x 2½ inches, or 9 x 5 x 3 inches. In a small bowl or cup, soften yeast in warm water; set aside.

In a large mixing bowl, measure 1 cup oats, salt, shortening, and molasses. Pour boiling water over mixture. Add 2 cups of flour, and beat well. Add yeast mixture and 2 beaten eggs, then add remaining flour to make a dough. Let rest 10 minutes.

Turn dough out onto a floured board and knead until smooth and elastic. Place dough in a large, greased bowl, turn to grease top, cover, and let rise in a warm place until doubled in bulk.

Sprinkle 2 tablespoons oats into prepared pans. Shape dough into 2 loaves and put in pans. Cover and let rise again until doubled.

Heat oven to 375 degrees. Brush tops of loaves with egg wash. Sprinkle tops of loaves with remaining 2 tablespoons oats. Bake at 375 degrees for 45 minutes to 1 hour. Check at 30 minutes. If loaves become too brown, cover with foil for the last few minutes of baking. Makes 2 loaves.

BEER MUFFINS
Vern

This is a breakfast treat.

4 cups Bisquick baking mix
½ cup plus 2 tbsp. sugar
1 can (12 oz.) beer, at room temperature

4 tbsp. butter or margarine
1 or 2 tbsp. cinnamon

Grease two 12-cup muffin tins (muffins stick to paper). Heat oven to 400 degrees.

In a large bowl, combine Bisquick, 2 tablespoons sugar, and beer; mix well. Beat vigorously for 2 minutes. Fill each muffin cup about half full. Bake for 15 minutes.

Melt butter or margarine in a small pan. Mix ½ cup sugar with cinnamon in a small bowl. Dip each muffin first in melted butter or margarine, then in sugar-cinnamon mixture. Serve hot. Makes 24 muffins.

KEEP-ON-HAND BRAN MUFFINS
Vern

"These are great!" says recipe tester Annabel DeCock of Eldridge, Iowa.

5 cups flour
3 cups sugar
5 tsp. baking soda
2 tsp. salt
1 cup chopped nuts or
  raisins (optional)

4 eggs
1 cup salad oil
1 qt. buttermilk
1 box (15 oz.) Raisin Bran
  cereal

In a large mixing bowl, measure flour, sugar, baking soda, and salt. Add nuts or raisins. In another large bowl, beat eggs. Add oil and buttermilk to eggs, then add to dry ingredients. Mix just until well blended, but do not beat. Stir in Raisin Bran cereal. Cover and store batter in a tightly covered container in the refrigerator. Batter will keep for up to six weeks in the refrigerator.

When ready to bake, heat oven to 400 degrees, and grease muffin tins. Remove as much dough as needed from storage container, and place in muffin tins, filling each cup half full. Bake at 400 degrees for 20 minutes. Makes 6 dozen large or 12 dozen small muffins.

Note: Muffins may be baked and frozen for up to six months.

FILLED COFFEE CAKE
Vern

½ cup shortening
¾ cup sugar
2 egg yolks, beaten
1½ cups flour
2 tsp. baking powder
½ tsp. salt
½ cup milk

1 tsp. vanilla

FILLING:
½ cup brown sugar
2 tbsp. flour
1½ tsp. cinnamon
½ cup finely chopped nuts

In a large bowl, cream shortening and sugar. Add beaten egg yolks. In a small bowl, sift flour with baking powder and salt. Add milk and flour mixture alternately to creamed mixture. Add vanilla.

Heat oven to 350 degrees. In a dry bowl, combine filling ingredients; mix well. Put half of batter in a greased 9 x 13 x 2-inch pan. Sprinkle with filling, then carefully spoon on remaining batter. Bake at 350 degrees for 25 to 30 minutes, or until a toothpick inserted in center comes out clean. Serve coffee cake hot. Makes 12 servings.

SOUR CREAM COFFEE CAKE
Vern

1 cup butter or margarine	1 tsp. baking powder
1¼ cups sugar	½ tsp. baking soda
1 tsp. vanilla	½ tsp. salt
2 eggs	1 cup sour cream
2 cups flour	

MIDDLE LAYER:

1½ tsp. cinnamon	3 tbsp. sugar

Grease a 9-cup Bundt pan. Heat oven to 350 degrees. In the large bowl of an electric mixer, cream butter or margarine, 1¼ cups sugar, vanilla, and eggs together with mixer until light and fluffy. In a medium-size bowl, sift flour, baking powder, baking soda, and salt together. Add sifted ingredients to creamed mixture alternately with sour cream. Pour half of mixture into prepared pan.

For the middle layer, mix cinnamon and 3 tablespoons sugar and sprinkle over top of batter. Spread remaining half of batter over the top. Bake at 350 degrees for about 1 hour, or until a toothpick inserted in center comes out clean. Remove from the pan immediately, and cool slightly on rack. While cake is still warm, spread with Confectioners' Sugar Glaze (recipe follows). Makes 14 to 16 servings.

CONFECTIONERS' SUGAR GLAZE

**1 tbsp. butter or
margarine, softened
½ cup milk**

**1 cup confectioners' sugar
½ tsp. vanilla**

Place softened butter or margarine in a small bowl. Alternately add milk and confectioners' sugar, mixing until smooth. Add vanilla and mix well. Brush on cake while it's still warm and enjoy!

Meat, Poultry, and Fish

Meats

SALT PORK
Elizabeth

These first three recipes were used when cooks were restricted to an open fire. Although we don't cook this way today, these recipes show how our ancestors prepared meat.

Use thin slices of thick side pork, clear white and streaked with lean. Hold one on a toasting fork before a brisk fire to grill. Have at hand a vessel (large pot) of cold water. Frequently immerse the salt pork while cooking to remove the extra fat. Put slices of cooked pork in a warming pan when done, and serve hot.

TO PRESERVE MEAT
BY DRY SALTING
Elizabeth

For dry rubbing or salting of meat and fish, heat the salt in a large skillet. Allow 2 pounds of coarse salt to 25 pounds of meat. Rub in salt with a heavy hand and place in pickling tub. A brine is soon formed by the salt absorbed in the juice of the meat. With this, the meat should be wetted every day and a different side turned down. In 10 to 12 days, it will be sufficiently cured.

TO PRESERVE MEAT
WITHOUT SALTING
Elizabeth

This was a common practice in the mid-1800s.

A joint can be held several days by hanging it with good ventilation and placing over it a cloth well moistened with apple cider vinegar. The vinegar cloth must be well soaked at least twice a day and should cover the meat well to keep away flies and insects.

FRIED LIVER AND ONIONS
Sara

On butchering days, the liver was the first part of the new meat to be used. It was soaked all day in salt brine. Usually, it was cut up and shared as a delicacy with family and neighbors.

1 lb. fresh liver
Flour or bread crumbs
Salt and pepper to taste

1 egg, beaten
3 tbsp. butter, melted
2 medium onions, sliced

Cut the liver into rather thin slices, ¼ to ½ inch thick. Roll each slice in flour or bread crumbs, season with salt and pepper, and dip in beaten egg.

In a skillet, fry the meat in melted butter. Cook for about 2 to 3 minutes, or until brown and crispy. Add onions last to heat through. Serves 4 or 5.

SHEPHERD'S PIE
Sara

For use with leftovers from steaks, roasts, or stews. The size of the dish depends on the amount of leftovers to be used.

ROOTS AND RECIPES

1½ to 2 cups chunked
   leftover steak, roast, or
   stew
2 cups mashed potatoes
   (leftover or fresh)

½ cup bread crumbs
Salt and pepper to taste
2 tbsp. butter, cut up
½ cup leftover gravy or
   canned stock

Heat oven to 350 degrees. Grind any remains of steaks, roasts, or stew meat or chop into bite-size pieces. Grease a baking vessel (dish or pan), and put in a layer of mashed potatoes, then a layer of meat and a layer of bread crumbs. Season with salt and pepper and bits of butter. Moisten with gravy or stock. Add another layer of potatoes. Dip a knife in milk and smooth over the top.

Bake, uncovered, at 350 degrees for 30 to 45 minutes, or until nicely brown.

HAM OR PORK BOILED DINNER
Lavina

On a busy wash day, Grandma put a chunk of ham hock in water on the back of the stove and let it simmer all morning while she worked. By noon, a delicious dinner was ready. This easily can be made today by cooking it for 3 to 4 hours on low heat, or in a slow cooker.

1 ham hock (3 lb.)
Water (to cover ham hock)
3 or 4 whole carrots

2 whole onions
3 or 4 whole potatoes
Salt and pepper to taste

Put the ham hock in a big kettle or saucepan and cover it with water. Let it come slowly to a boil. Skim off foam. Cook, covered, for about 3 hours. Remove ham hock from liquid; cut off fat and bones, and return meat to kettle. Cover and continue to simmer over low heat while preparing vegetables.

Quarter the vegetables and add to the kettle during the last hour of cooking. Add salt and pepper, as desired. Cook on low heat for a total of 3 to 4 hours, until meat and vegetables are tender. Serves 4.

POT ROAST
Lavina

3 to 4 lb. arm or blade pot
  roast of beef
3 tbsp. shortening
¾ cup water
1 tsp. salt
¼ tsp. pepper
6 medium-size potatoes,
  peeled

6 medium-size carrots
6 medium-size onions
1 cup tomato juice
1 small head cabbage, cut
  in wedges (optional)
2 tbsp. flour

On top of the stove, brown the pot roast on all sides in hot shortening in a heavy dutch oven on low heat. Add ½ cup of the water and salt and pepper. Cover and simmer for 2½ hours, adding more water, about ½ cup, if needed. Add potatoes, carrots, onions, and tomato juice. Cover and cook for 20 minutes, then add cabbage, cover, and cook for 15 minutes more. Remove meat and vegetables with a slotted spoon. Keep warm.

For the gravy, mix the flour in ¼ cup water and slowly add it to the boiling liquid. Cook and stir until thickened. Serves 6.

Note: Unless the potatoes, carrots, and onions are large, cook them whole.

INDIVIDUAL HAM LOAVES
Vern

This recipe makes 36 to 40 small loaves—enough to feed a crowd—and is popular at large social events. It is an ideal recipe to make, divide into packages, and freeze for extended use. Co-author Connie Heckert made this recipe one Christmas and gave it to family and neighbors, just as her mother, a lifelong Iowa resident, used to give gifts of freshly made butter or strawberry jam.

5 lb. ground smoked ham
3 lb. lean ground beef
10 eggs
1 box (18 oz.) corn flakes

1½ qt. tomato juice
2 tsp. sage
2 tsp. celery salt

Heat oven to 350 degrees. In a large bowl, gently mix all ingredients together and form into little loaves.

Place the little loaves side by side on an ungreased jelly-roll pan, and bake, uncovered, at 350 degrees for 1 hour. Makes about 40 individual ham loaves.

Note: These little loaves can be made ahead of time, wrapped, and frozen unbaked. Remove from freezer and thaw in refrigerator before baking. Or, bake from frozen state, adding about 15 to 20 minutes to baking time.

BARBECUED PORK CHOPS
Vern

Because there's no need to brown the chops first, this recipe is easy to prepare.

4 pork chops, each about
   ¾ inch thick
½ cup brown sugar

½ cup ketchup
1 tbsp. dry mustard
Salt to taste

Heat oven to 350 degrees. Place pork chops in a single layer in a baking dish. Mix remaining ingredients and spread over chops, reserving some of the sauce to heat and pour over the pork chops at serving time.

Bake, covered, at 350 degrees for 30 minutes. Uncover, baste chops, and bake another 30 to 45 minutes, until chops are tender and done. Heat reserved sauce in a small pan, and pour over pork chops just before serving. Serves 4.

Note: For thinner pork chops, reduce the baking time.

PORK CHOPS AND RICE

Vern

4 pork chops, each about
   ¾ inch thick
1 tbsp. vegetable
   shortening, melted
4 tbsp. uncooked rice

4 tbsp. chopped onion
1 can (10¾ oz.) tomato
   soup
Water (as needed)

In a skillet, brown pork chops on both sides in melted shortening. Put 1 tablespoon of raw rice on top of each chop. Add 1 tablespoon chopped onion to each chop. Pour tomato soup over all. Add just enough water to cover the bottom of the skillet. Cover and simmer on top of range until chops are tender, about 45 to 60 minutes. Serves 4.

Poultry

CHICKEN AND DUMPLINGS
Elizabeth Jane

1 whole chicken (hen), about 3 lb.	2 eggs
3 cups flour	1 tbsp. butter, melted
4 tsp. baking powder	1 cup milk (approximately)
½ tsp. salt	1 tbsp. flour (for gravy)
	1 tbsp. water (for gravy)

In a large, covered kettle, simmer the chicken in water to cover, until tender, about 1 hour. Remove chicken from broth, and keep both chicken and broth warm.

In a mixing bowl, sift the 3 cups flour, baking powder, and salt together. In a small bowl or cup, beat eggs until light and fluffy. Add beaten eggs, melted butter, and enough milk to flour mixture to make a soft dough.

Bring broth in kettle to boiling. Drop dough by tablespoonful into boiling broth. Cook, uncovered, for about 20 minutes, carefully turning each dumpling once. Remove dumplings from broth with a slotted spoon. Keep warm.

If desired, make gravy with broth. Mix 1 tablespoon flour with 1 tablespoon water in a small saucepan and slowly stir in 1 cup broth. Cook and stir until gravy thickens. Serve dumplings with chicken and gravy. Serves 6.

CHICKEN AND DRESSING BAKE
Vern

1 pkg. (8 oz.) herb dressing mix	2 cups chicken broth
2 tbsp. diced onion	2 eggs, well beaten
1 can (10¾ oz.) condensed cream of chicken soup	2½ cups diced cooked chicken
	½ cup milk
	2 tbsp. diced pimiento

Heat oven to 350 degrees. In a bowl, combine the stuffing mix with onion, half of the can of soup, chicken broth, and beaten eggs; mix well. Grease a 9 x 13 x 2-inch baking dish. Spread stuffing mixture on bottom of dish. Add the diced chicken.

In a small bowl, mix remaining soup with milk and pimiento. Pour over the chicken and dressing. Bake, uncovered, at 350 degrees for 45 minutes, or until dressing is cooked and set. Makes 6 generous servings.

CHICKEN POT PIE
Vern

2 or 3 ribs celery
1 chicken (hen), 3 to 4 lb.
1 medium onion, chopped
1 tsp. salt
½ cup butter, melted
½ cup flour
1 cup chopped celery

4 carrots, cubed
2 cups cubed cooked
   potatoes
1 pkg. (10 oz.) frozen peas
1 recipe Jessie's or Vern's
   Pie Crust (see index)

Chop 2 or 3 ribs of celery. Put chicken, celery, onion, and salt in a large kettle with enough water to cover. Bring to a boil, reduce heat to low, cover, and cook until chicken is tender, about 1½ to 2 hours (or use a slow cooker).

Remove from heat and set aside to cool. When cool enough to handle, remove chicken from broth. Bone the chicken and cut meat into bite-size pieces. Set chicken meat aside. Strain celery and onion from broth. Reserve 2 cups of the broth. Discard celery and onion.

In a saucepan, mix melted butter with flour and slowly stir in the 2 cups chicken broth. Bring to a boil and cook, stirring constantly, for 1 minute.

In another saucepan, cover and cook 1 cup chopped celery, carrots, potatoes, and peas in water to cover until vegetables are tender, about 15 minutes. Drain and add vegetables to chicken broth mixture, along with the chicken meat. Mix well.

Preheat oven to 375 degrees. Make a single pie crust and set aside (see index for Jessie's or Vern's pie crust). Grease a 2-quart casserole. Place chicken mixture in casserole and cover with pie crust. Slit holes in the crust to allow steam to escape. Bake at 375 degrees for 35 to 45 minutes, until golden brown. Serves 6.

OVEN CHICKEN FRY
Vern

This is easy to do for a crowd, and it's the best chicken you ever ate!

1 chicken, cut up
1 cup margarine or butter, melted

1 cup flour (for coating)
Salt and pepper to taste

Heat oven to 350 degrees. Dip chicken pieces in the melted butter, then roll in flour. Line a jelly-roll pan with foil for easy cleaning. Lay the prepared chicken in a single layer on the foil, but do not allow the pieces to touch each other. Pour any remaining butter over the chicken. Sprinkle with salt and pepper.

Bake, uncovered, at 350 degrees for 1 hour. Turn the chicken once halfway through baking time. Serves 4 to 6.

CHICKEN BREASTS SUPREME
Vern

2½ cups seasoned
   croutons
2 tsp. sage
1½ tbsp. onion flakes
1 egg, beaten
Chicken bouillon to make
   1¼ cups liquid
6 slices dried beef

6 chicken breast halves,
   boned, skinned, and
   flattened
12 slices bacon
1 can (10¾ oz.) cream of
   mushroom soup
1 carton (8 oz.) sour cream

In a large mixing bowl, combine the croutons, sage, onion flakes, egg, and bouillon. Place dried beef and 3 tablespoons stuffing in the center of each breast. Roll up tightly. Secure with toothpicks. Wrap two slices of bacon around each roll. Place in a greased 9 x 13 x 2-inch baking dish, making sure the chicken rolls are not touching.

Heat oven to 325 degrees. In a small bowl, combine soup and sour cream; mix well. Pour over chicken. Cover and bake at 325 degrees for 1 hour. Uncover and bake 30 minutes longer to brown. Serves 6.

CHICKEN ROLL-UPS
Vern

6 chicken breast halves,
boned, skinned, and
flattened
1 pkg. (8 oz.) cream
cheese, softened

Chopped chives (optional)
6 slices bacon
Hot cooked rice

Heat oven to 350 degrees. Spread the chicken breasts with the cream cheese and sprinkle with chopped chives. Roll up. Wind a bacon strip around each roll. Place in a greased 9 x 13 x 2-inch baking dish, making sure sides of rolls are not touching. Bake, uncovered, at 350 degrees for 45 minutes to 1 hour, or until cheese mixture is bubbly. Serve with hot cooked rice. Serves 6.

CHICKEN DIVAN
Vern

4 or 5 chicken breasts (or
enough to make 3 cups
cut-up chicken)
1 pkg. (1 lb.) frozen
broccoli
2 cans (10¾ oz. each)
cream of chicken soup
1 cup real mayonnaise

½ tsp. lemon juice
½ tsp. curry powder
(optional)
1 cup grated cheese
(mozzarella, provolone,
or Swiss)
Dash paprika

Bake or poach the chicken breasts until done; cut off enough chicken meat to make 3 cups. Cook broccoli according to package directions and drain. Use broccoli spears if using a 9 x 13 x 2-inch baking dish or chopped broccoli for a 2-quart casserole. Heat oven to 350 degrees.

Arrange the broccoli in the bottom of the dish, and layer the cooked chicken pieces on top. Combine the soup, mayonnaise, lemon juice, and curry powder. Pour mixture over the chicken, then top with grated cheese and sprinkle with paprika. Bake, uncovered, at 350 degrees for 30 to 45 minutes, until brown. Serves 4 to 6.

Fish

SALMON SUPPER
Vern

2 tbsp. butter
2 tbsp. flour
2 cups milk
1 can (15 oz.) salmon,
   drained and flaked

1 cup cooked or leftover
   vegetables (peas, lima
   beans, green beans, or
   corn)
2 cups mashed potatoes

Heat oven to 350 degrees. In a saucepan, melt the butter, stir in flour, and cook until mixture bubbles. Over low heat, slowly add milk, stirring constantly until mixture thickens to a white sauce. Stir in the salmon and any cooked vegetables.

Pour mixture into a greased 9-inch pie plate. Cover with mashed potatoes. Bake, uncovered, at 350 degrees until brown, about 30 minutes. Serves 4.

SALMON LOAF
Vern

1 can (15 oz.) salmon,
   drained and flaked
1 tbsp. butter, melted
½ cup bread crumbs
2 or 3 ribs celery, chopped

1 small onion, chopped
2 eggs, beaten lightly
2 tbsp. lemon juice
¼ tsp. salt (optional)
⅛ tsp. pepper

Heat oven to 350 degrees. In a mixing bowl, combine salmon, butter, crumbs, celery, onion, eggs, lemon juice, salt, and pepper; mix well. Put in a buttered 1-quart casserole and set in a shallow pan. Place in oven and carefully fill shallow pan with hot water halfway to the top of the casserole. Bake, uncovered, at 350 degrees for 1 hour, refilling the pan with hot water as needed. Serves 4.

Note: Salmon Loaf often is served with creamed peas, on top or on the side, which adds color and flavor.

SALMON PATTIES
Vern

1 can (15 oz.) salmon,
drained and flaked
¾ cup mashed potatoes
1 onion, chopped
1 egg, well beaten
½ cup peas
¼ cup finely diced celery
⅓ cup flour (approximately)

Salt to taste (optional)
Pepper to taste
2 eggs, well beaten
(optional)
Bread crumbs (optional)
Fat (for frying)

In a mixing bowl, combine salmon, mashed potatoes, chopped onion, and 1 well-beaten egg; mix well. Add the peas and celery, mixing carefully so as not to mash peas. Add about ⅓ cup of flour and salt and pepper to taste. Form mixture into 5 patties.

If desired, dip each patty in 2 well-beaten eggs, then in bread crumbs. In a skillet, fry patties in hot fat until brown on both sides. Serves 5.

Gravies

MILK GRAVY
Elizabeth

This gravy can be made after frying chicken, pork chops, or ham.

2 tbsp. meat drippings	**Salt to taste**
2 tbsp. flour	**Pepper to taste**
2 or 3 cups sweet milk	

In the same pan used for frying chicken or meat, over low heat, add flour to the drippings and stir until smooth. Slowly stir in milk, cooking until gravy reaches desired thickness. Makes 2 to 3 cups gravy.

BROWN GRAVY
Lavina

This gravy goes well with a beef or pork roast.

Meat drippings	**Salt to taste**
2½ cups water	**Pepper to taste**
2 tbsp. flour	

Add 2 cups of water to brown drippings in the roasting pan. Bring to a boil. In a measuring cup, blend flour with remaining ½ cup water and mix until smooth. Slowly add to boiling liquid in roasting pan. Over low heat, stir and cook until mixture is thick, adding more water if gravy needs to be thinned. Makes approximately 2½ cups gravy.

Main Dishes and Casseroles

HOMEMADE NOODLES
Jessie

My mother prepared these to go with stewed chicken on Sundays.

3 eggs	**1½ to 2 cups flour**
Salt	**Chicken broth**

In a mixing bowl, beat the eggs and sprinkle on a little bit of salt. Add flour with a spoon until thick; then continue to add flour (about ½ cup) with your hand. When you can form a ball with the dough, roll out tissue-thin on a floured board and leave until almost dry, about 1 hour. Cut in strips and pull apart. Allow to finish drying on a rack or on wax paper or paper toweling.

Cook in boiling chicken broth until tender, or until noodles can be cut easily with a fork on the edge of the pan. Serves 6.

MACARONI AND CHEESE
Jessie

This is a simple, basic recipe for family.

1 cup uncooked macaroni	**Salt**
½ lb. American cheese,	**Pepper**
cubed	**1 cup grated American**
½ cup milk	**cheese**
1 cup buttered cracker or	
bread crumbs	

Cook macaroni according to package directions; drain and rinse. Melt the ½ pound American cheese and milk in the top of a double boiler over hot, but not boiling water. Stir constantly until mixture thickens. Heat oven to 400 degrees.

Place cooked macaroni in a greased 1-quart baking dish, sprinkle with salt and pepper to taste, and cover with the cheese sauce. Stir to mix well. Top with buttered crumbs and grated cheese.

Bake, uncovered, until brown on top, about 30 to 45 minutes. Serves 8.

CREAMED HAMBURGER
Vern

This is the very first recipe I collected as a young bride.

1 lb. ground beef	**1 heaping tbsp. flour**
1 large onion, chopped	**2 to 3 cups milk**

In a skillet, brown the ground beef with plenty of onions. Drain off excess fat. When meat is brown, sprinkle on the flour and cook and stir until well blended. Stir in cold milk to the thickness you desire; cook until hot but not boiling. Serve on mashed potatoes, rice, or toast. Serves 6 to 8.

Note: Chipped beef, ham, chicken, or turkey, or a combination of these may be substituted for ground beef.

PORK SAUSAGE, APPLES, AND SWEET POTATOES
Jessie

¾ lb. bulk pork sausage	**½ cup cold water**
4 sweet potatoes	**2 tbsp. white sugar**
6 apples	**½ tsp. salt**
1 tbsp. flour	**1 tbsp. sausage drippings**

Shape sausage into small balls. In a skillet, fry sausage balls until browned on all sides; drain and reserve the fat. Peel and slice the sweet potatoes and apples.

Heat oven to 375 degrees. In a 2-quart casserole or a 9 x 13 x 2-inch baking dish (it will be full), arrange the sausage balls, apples, and sweet potatoes in layers. In a small bowl, stir flour into cold water; mix well. Add sugar, salt, and 1 tablespoon sausage drippings, blending well. Pour over top layer in casserole. Cover and bake at 375 degrees for 45 minutes. Serves 8.

EASY STROGANOFF BAKE
Vern

1½ lb. ground beef
2 tbsp. onion flakes
¼ tsp. garlic powder
¼ tsp. salt (optional)
¼ tsp. pepper

1 can (10¾ oz.) vegetable-
  beef soup
½ cup milk
1 cup sour cream

In a skillet, brown the ground beef, onion flakes, garlic powder, salt, and pepper. Drain off excess fat. Stir in soup. Cook slowly for 15 minutes. Blend in the milk and sour cream, cooking over low heat until blended. Do not boil.

Heat oven to 475 degrees. Pour into a greased 9-inch square pan and bake, uncovered, for 20 minutes. Serve with biscuits or toast or over noodles. Serves 6 to 8.

BARBECUED BEANS AND BEEF
Vern

This is great for a cookout! Historically, cooks put a dish like this in a kettle on the back burner to cook slowly during wash day or when they had other big tasks.

1 lb. ground beef
1 lb. bacon, cut in pieces
1 onion, chopped
2 cans (16 oz. each) kid-
  ney beans, undrained
2 cans (16 oz. each) pork
  and beans, undrained
2 cans (15 oz. each) butter
  beans, undrained

½ cup ketchup
½ cup barbecue sauce
1 tsp. salt (optional)
4 tbsp. salad-style mustard
4 tbsp. molasses
1 tsp. chili powder

In a skillet, brown ground beef and bacon pieces; add chopped onion and cook slightly. Drain well and set aside. In a large bowl, combine beans with their liquid, ketchup, barbecue sauce, salt, mustard, molasses, and chili powder; mix well.

Heat oven to 350 degrees. Combine ground beef and bean mixtures and pour into a greased 9 x 13 x 2-inch baking dish. Bake, uncovered, for 1 hour, or until beans are tender, or cook all day on low setting in a slow cooker. The ingredients fill a 3½-quart slow cooker and may bubble over if the entire recipe is cooked all at once. Watch it carefully. Serves 12 to 15.

BARBECUED MEATBALLS
Vern

2 lb. lean ground beef
1 cup uncooked oats
1 cup milk
1½ cups ketchup
3 tbsp. vinegar

4½ tbsp. Worcestershire
  sauce
2 tbsp. chopped onion
3 tbsp. brown sugar

In a mixing bowl, combine the beef, oats, and milk; mix well, then form into small balls. Do not brown. Place in a lightly greased 9 x 13 x 2-inch baking pan.

Heat oven to 275 degrees. In a small bowl, combine the remaining ingredients, mix well, and pour over meatballs. Bake, covered, at 275 degrees for 2 hours. Turn once. These will brown nicely without browning the meat first. Makes 18 to 20 meatballs.

BARBECUED BEEF FOR SANDWICHES
Vern

1 lb. ground beef
1 tsp. drippings
1 large onion, chopped
  fine
1 green pepper, chopped
  fine

1 tbsp. sugar
2 tbsp. prepared mustard
1 tbsp. vinegar
1 tsp. salt (or less)
¾ cup ketchup

In a skillet, brown meat, stirring until crumbly; remove beef and drain off fat. Return 1 teaspoon drippings to skillet; stir in all other ingredients and beef. Cover and simmer for 30 minutes. Serve on buns. Makes 6 to 8 sandwiches.

HEAVENLY HASH
Vern

6 slices bacon, diced
1 onion, chopped
1½ lb. ground beef
1 pkg. (6 to 8 oz.) noodles,
  cooked and drained
1 pkg. (10 oz.) frozen peas
1 can (8 oz.) sliced
  mushrooms, drained

2 cans (10¾ oz. each)
  tomato soup
1 cup cracker crumbs
1 cup grated cheddar
  cheese (optional)

In a skillet, cook the diced bacon and onion until brown. Add the ground beef, brown, then drain off excess fat. In a bowl, combine ground beef mixture with cooked noodles, peas, mushrooms, and tomato soup; blend well.

Heat oven to 350 degrees. Place mixture in a 9 x 13 x 2-inch baking dish or a large casserole. Top with cracker crumbs and grated cheese. Bake, uncovered, at 350 degrees for 45 to 60 minutes. Serves 8 to 10.

HAMBURGER SUPPER PIE
Vern

1 lb. ground beef
½ cup chopped onion
1 tbsp. shortening
2 tsp. chili powder
1 tsp. salt

1 tbsp. Worcestershire
  sauce
1 cup canned tomatoes
1 cup kidney beans,
  drained

CORNBREAD BATTER:

2 eggs, well beaten
½ cup sugar
1 cup milk
1 cup flour

1 cup cornmeal
4 tsp. baking powder
½ tsp. salt
3 tbsp. melted shortening

In a skillet, brown the ground beef and onion in the shortening. Drain off excess fat. Add chili powder, salt, Worcestershire sauce, and tomatoes; mix well. Simmer, uncovered, for 15 minutes. Stir in kidney beans.

Heat oven to 425 degrees. To make cornbread batter, beat eggs and add sugar in a mixing bowl. Stir in the milk, and gradually add dry ingredients. Add melted shortening. Mix well, but do not overmix batter. Pour beef mixture into a 1½-quart casserole. Top with cornbread batter, spreading batter carefully with a knife. Bake for 30 minutes, or until cornbread is golden brown and tests done with a toothpick inserted near the center. Serves 10 easily.

Note: To make cornbread alone, combine ingredients as instructed, and bake in a greased 8- or 9-inch pan at 400 degrees for 20 minutes, or until a wooden pick inserted near the center comes out clean.

HAM STRATA
Vern

2 cups chopped celery
2 tbsp. butter or
   margarine
8 slices white bread, crusts
   removed
1 cup grated cheddar
   cheese

2 cups diced ham
2 cups milk
4 eggs, beaten
2 tbsp. onion flakes
Dash salt
Dash pepper

In a skillet or saucepan, cook celery in butter or margarine until tender. Drain off excess butter or margarine. Cut a circle from each slice of bread, then crumble remaining bread in a greased 8 x 12-inch baking dish. Sprinkle with cheese. Cover with cooked celery and diced ham. Top with the bread circles.

Heat oven to 350 degrees. In a small bowl, mix milk, eggs, onion flakes, salt, and pepper, and pour over all. Refrigerate for 1 hour. Bake, uncovered, at 350 degrees for 1 hour, or until mixture is firm and top is golden brown. Serves 8.

HAM A LA KING
Vern

1 cup chopped green
   pepper
2 tbsp. butter or
   margarine, melted
2 tbsp. flour
½ cup rich cream
2 cans (4 oz. each) sliced
   mushrooms (drain and
   reserve liquid)

Milk (as needed)
2 eggs, beaten
2 cups cubed ham
1 jar (4 oz.) pimientos,
   drained and chopped
1 tsp. lemon juice
Salt to taste
Pepper to taste

In a skillet, cook chopped green pepper in melted butter until soft, but not brown. Blend flour into the green peppers. Stir in cream. Drain liquid from mushrooms and add enough milk to the mushroom liquid to make 1 cup. In a small bowl, add a little of the milk mixture to the beaten eggs, then add to green pepper mixture in the skillet. Cook until the mixture is thick.

Stir in remaining milk mixture, mushrooms, ham, pimientos, lemon juice, salt, and pepper. Heat through to serving temperature. Serve on toast, in patty shells, or on mashed potatoes. Serves 6 to 8.

MACARONI AND CHICKEN, HAM, OR TURKEY
Vern

This is especially good as an inexpensive, prepare-ahead dish for potluck dinners. It can be refrigerated overnight and baked the day of serving.

7 oz. uncooked macaroni
2 cups diced cooked
   chicken, ham, or
   turkey
2 cups milk
1 can (10¾ oz.) cream of
   chicken soup

1 can (10¾ oz.) cream of
   mushroom soup
½ lb. Velveeta cheese,
   cubed
1 small onion, diced
1 jar (4 oz.) pimientos,
   drained and chopped

In a large bowl, combine uncooked maracroni, diced cooked chicken, milk, soups, cubed cheese, diced onion, and chopped pimientos. Mix well. Pour into a 1-quart baking dish or casserole. Cover and refrigerate overnight.

Heat oven to 350 degrees. Remove casserole from refrigerator; stir well. Bake, uncovered, for 1 hour and 15 minutes. Serves 8 generously.

TUNA AU GRATIN
Vern

CRUST:

1½ cups sifted flour	**½ cup margarine**
½ tsp. salt	**4 to 5 tbsp. cold water**

TUNA FILLING:

1 can (10¾ oz.) cream of mushroom soup	**2 cans (6½ oz. each) tuna, drained and flaked**
¼ cup milk	**1 jar (4 oz.) chopped pimientos, drained**
2 tbsp. flour	
2 tbsp. onion flakes	**1 cup shredded American cheese**
1 pkg. (1½ cups) frozen peas	

Heat the oven to 450 degrees. In a bowl, mix flour and salt. With a pastry blender or two forks, cut in margarine until fine particles form. Sprinkle water over while mixing with a fork until dough holds together. Roll pastry out on a lightly floured board to fit a 9-inch pie pan. Place loosely in pan. Trim pastry and flute edges. Prick the bottom of pastry shell with a fork, then bake the crust at 450 degrees for about 12 minutes, until lightly browned.

Reduce oven temperature to 425 degrees. In a saucepan, combine soup, milk, flour, and onion flakes; mix well. Cook over low heat, stirring constantly, until thick. In a microwave oven, cook peas slightly in a microwave-safe dish with a small amount of water, or in a saucepan according to package directions. Stir peas, tuna, and pimientos into soup mixture. Bring to a boil, then remove from heat.

Turn hot filling into the baked pie shell. Sprinkle shredded cheese over the filling. Bake at 425 degrees for 15 minutes, or until brown. Serves 6 to 8.

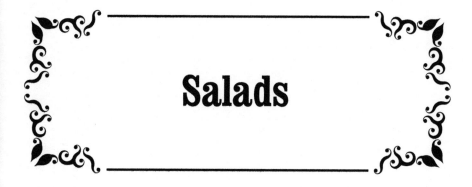

Salads

WILTED LETTUCE SALAD
Sarah

When leaf lettuce was ready to be picked from the garden, it was a welcome change in the menu. Spinach may be substituted for lettuce.

6 slices bacon or salt pork
6 to 8 cups leaf lettuce in
   bite-size pieces
¼ cup vinegar

4 tsp. sugar
1 tbsp. water
3 hard-cooked eggs,
   chopped (optional)

In a skillet, fry bacon or salt pork until very crisp. Do not drain; leave the fat in the skillet. Drain bacon slices on paper toweling and crumble; set aside. If using salt pork, drain on paper toweling and dice; set aside.

Wash lettuce well, drain, and dry with paper toweling. Chop lettuce into bite-size pieces to measure 6 to 8 cups. Place in a salad bowl. In the skillet, add the vinegar, sugar, and water to the fat. Bring to boil, reduce heat to low; cook and stir until mixture is well blended. Pour over the lettuce, add crumbled bacon or diced salt pork, and garnish with hard-cooked eggs. Serves 6 to 8.

CABBAGE SLAW
Elizabeth Jane

1 small head fresh cabbage
Salt to taste
2 tbsp. sweet cream

2 tbsp. sugar
4 tbsp. vinegar

In a mixing bowl, shred fresh cabbage and season with salt. In a small bowl or cup, mix together sweet cream, sugar, and vinegar. Pour dressing over the cabbage and stir well. Serve in a glass bowl. Serves 8.

CUCUMBERS IN SOUR CREAM

Lavina

2 long cucumbers	**¼ tsp. dill weed**
1 cup sour cream	**3 tbsp. vinegar**
½ tsp. salt	

Wash the cucumbers and peel or, if desired, leave skins on and scrape with a fork to add a decorative touch. With the tines, run the fork the length of the cucumber, then continue making rows until the entire cucumber is covered. Slice and set aside.

In a bowl, blend the sour cream, salt, dill weed, and vinegar. Stir in cucumbers, gently mixing well. Place in a container with a tight-fitting lid. Cover and refrigerate for 24 hours before serving. Makes 4 to 6 servings.

POTATO SALAD

Jessie

Water (to cover potatoes)	**¼ cup chopped red or**
½ tsp. salt	**green pepper (optional)**
5 or 6 medium-size	**½ to 1 cup homemade**
potatoes	**salad dressing (recipe**
4 hard-cooked eggs,	**follows) or commercial**
chopped	**dressing**
1 cup chopped celery	**Salt and pepper to taste**
½ cup chopped onion	

In a kettle or saucepan, bring to boiling enough water to cover potatoes. Add ½ teaspoon salt and potatoes. Return to a boil, reduce heat, cover, and cook over moderate heat until potatoes are tender, about 30 to 35 minutes. Drain and cool.

Cut potatoes into cubes. Place in a mixing bowl and gently stir in chopped eggs, celery, onion, and red or green pepper, if desired. Add enough salad dressing to cover well. Mix gently, adding salt and pepper to taste. Serves 8.

HOMEMADE SALAD DRESSING

2 eggs, beaten
2 tbsp. sugar
2 tbsp. flour
1 tsp. dry mustard

Dash salt (optional)
Pepper to taste
1 cup water
¼ cup cider vinegar

In a small bowl, beat the eggs until light and fluffy. Add sugar, flour, dry mustard, salt, and pepper, blending thoroughly. Pour into a small saucepan and add water and cider vinegar, stirring to mix well. Cook over medium heat until thick. Remove from heat and cool.

Note: Be sure the ingredients of the salad are well-coated with dressing for best flavor.

APPLES AND PEANUTS SALAD
Vern

Frequently, when ladies are planning luncheons for a crowd, someone calls me to ask for a good dish to serve. This recipe was chosen for a spring luncheon and style show at Asbury Methodist Church in Bettendorf, Iowa, in 1989.

1 can (8 oz.) crushed
  pineapple
½ cup sugar
1 tbsp. flour
2 tbsp. vinegar
1 egg
4 cups unpeeled coarsely
  chopped red apples
  (such as Red Delicious)

½ cup chopped celery
1 cup salted peanuts
1 container (8 oz.) frozen
  whipped topping,
  thawed

Drain the juice from the crushed pineapple into a saucepan and reserve the fruit. Mix sugar and flour. Add sugar-flour mixture and vinegar to the juice in the saucepan. Beat the egg and add to the mixture, mixing thoroughly. Cook, stirring constantly, over low heat until thick. Remove from heat and cool.

In a bowl, combine the apples, celery, and reserved crushed pineapple. Pour cooled dressing over the mixture. Fold in peanuts and whipped topping. Serves 8 to 10.

DELECTABLE FROZEN SALAD
Vern

The party tea cake size of this frozen salad is great for a buffet or ladies' salad luncheon.

2 cups sour cream	**¼ cup chopped**
¾ cup sugar	**maraschino cherries**
2 tbsp. lemon juice	**½ cup chopped mixed nuts**
1 can (20 oz.) crushed	**1 ripe banana, sliced**
pineapple, drained	

In a bowl, combine all ingredients; mix gently but thoroughly. Spoon mixture into tea cake-size or muffin baking paper cups, filling each two-thirds full. Freeze until firm. Remove from freezer about 10 minutes before serving. Sprinkle with chopped nuts or a piece of a maraschino cherry for garnish. Makes equivalent of 36 tea cakes or 12 to 14 muffins.

FROZEN CHERRY SALAD
Vern

This salad is especially pretty for Christmas and Valentine's Day.

1 cup sour cream	**1 can (20 oz.) crushed**
1 pkg. (8 oz.) cream	**pineapple, drained**
cheese, softened	**1 can (11 oz.) mandarin**
¼ cup sugar	**oranges, drained**
Dash salt	**2 cups miniature**
1 can (17 oz.) dark sweet	**marshmallows**
cherries, drained	**¼ cup chopped pecans**

In a large bowl, mix the sour cream and cream cheese together, beating until well blended and smooth. Stir in sugar and salt, blending well. Add drained cherries, pineapple, mandarin oranges, marshmallows, and pecans. Mix well. Pour into a 9 x 13 x 2-inch dish or pan. Freeze overnight. Remove from freezer about 10 minutes before serving. Cut in squares to serve. Serves 15.

SPRING FRUIT SALAD

Vern

1 small head iceberg
  lettuce
3 cups fresh, frozen, or
  canned pineapple
  chunks
3 cups halved fresh
  strawberries

1 cup seedless grape
  halves
½ cup chopped celery
1 cup drained mandarin
  oranges (optional)

COCONUT SOUR CREAM DRESSING:

1 cup sour cream
4 tsp. lemon juice
1 tsp. prepared mustard

½ tsp. salt
¼ cup flaked coconut

Core, rinse, and drain lettuce; pat dry with paper toweling and cut into bite-size pieces to make 4 cups. Turn into a chilled bowl. Fold in pineapple, strawberries, grapes, celery, and mandarin oranges. In a bowl, combine sour cream, lemon juice, mustard, and salt; blend well. Fold in flaked coconut.

When ready to serve, top salad with Coconut Sour Cream Dressing. Serves 4.

SHRIMP SALAD
Vern

2 pkg. (7 oz. each) small
   shell macaroni (plain or
   fancy)
1 head cauliflower
½ cup chopped celery
1 medium onion, chopped
3 large dill pickles,
   chopped
5 hard-cooked eggs,
   chopped

12 oz. canned shrimp or
   half shrimp and half
   crabmeat, rinsed and
   chopped
1 qt. salad dressing
1 bottle (12 oz.) chili
   sauce
1½ tbsp. Worcestershire
   sauce

Cook shell macaroni according to package directions; drain. Cool in a large bowl. Bring to full boil a pan of water large enough to hold the head of cauliflower. Cover and steam the head of cauliflower in boiling water for 3 minutes. Cool and chop. Add chopped cauliflower to the macaroni. Add chopped celery, onion, pickles, eggs, and shrimp or shrimp and crabmeat combination, stirring to mix well.

Combine salad dressing, chili sauce, and Worcestershire sauce, then add it to the salad mixture and blend well. Cover and refrigerate. Keeps well for several days. Serves 16.

TOSSED SALAD
WITH MANDARIN ORANGES
Vern

Combine ingredients for the dressing early in the day or a day in advance, and refrigerate.

¼ cup salad oil
2 tbsp. tarragon vinegar
2 tbsp. sugar
½ tsp. salt
1 large head lettuce (or equivalent greens)
1 cup chopped celery
4 green onions, chopped

1 avocado, peeled, pitted, and diced (or 1 cucumber, sliced thin)
1 can (11 oz.) mandarin oranges, drained
Freshly ground pepper to taste

In a small bowl, combine oil, vinegar, sugar, and salt; mix well.

In a mixing bowl, tear lettuce into bite-sized pieces and add celery, onions, avocado or cucumber, and oranges. Add dressing to salad mixture and toss lightly. Add freshly ground pepper, if desired. Serves 6 to 8.

TWO BEAN SALAD
Vern

Prepare dressing ahead of time and chill it before serving.

2 tsp. sugar
2 tsp. wine vinegar
½ tsp. salt
¼ tsp. prepared mustard
¼ tsp. Worcestershire sauce
Pepper to taste
½ cup plain yogurt
2 cans (16 oz. each) green beans, drained

1 can (16 oz.) kidney beans, drained
2 hard-cooked eggs, chopped
½ cup chopped celery
¼ cup chopped sweet pickle
¼ cup chopped onions
½ cup chopped fresh mushrooms

In a small bowl, combine sugar, vinegar, ¼ teaspoon salt, mustard, Worcestershire sauce, and pepper; mix well. Stir in yogurt, blending thoroughly. Chill.

In a mixing bowl, combine drained green beans, kidney beans, chopped eggs, celery, pickle, onions, mushrooms, and remaining ¼ teaspoon salt, mixing gently but thoroughly. Add desired amount of dressing, toss gently, and chill. Serves 6.

PEA SALAD
Vern

1 bag (16 oz.) frozen peas
(do not thaw)
1 cup chopped celery
2 small green onions,
chopped
¾ cup mayonnaise

1 tbsp. lemon juice
1 tsp. soy sauce
1 can (3 oz.) chow mein
noodles
½ cup slivered almonds

In a bowl, mix peas, celery, green onions, mayonnaise, lemon juice, and soy sauce. Store in the refrigerator until ready to serve. Before serving, blend in the chow mein noodles and slivered almonds. Serves 6 to 8.

BROCCOLI CRUNCH SALAD
Vern

1 lb. bacon
1 full head broccoli
½ cup chopped red onions
¼ cup raisins

1 cup light salad dressing
2 tbsp. red wine vinegar
Scant ½ cup sugar

Cut up bacon with kitchen scissors or knife. In a skillet, fry until golden crisp. Drain on paper toweling and cool. Set aside. Wash broccoli and chop florets into bite-size pieces. In a medium-sized bowl, combine broccoli, bacon, red onions, and raisins.

In a small bowl, combine salad dressing, red wine vinegar, and sugar. Blend well. Add to broccoli mixture. Mix well, and chill before serving. Serves 6 to 8.

IOWA WINTER SALAD
Vern

4 egg yolks
4 tbsp. vinegar
4 tbsp. sugar
¼ lb. gumdrops (no
   licorice)
½ lb. marshmallows
   (miniature or regular,
   chopped)

1 can (20 oz.) pineapple
   chunks, drained
¼ cup drained maraschino
   cherries
¾ cup chopped nuts
1 container (8 oz.) frozen
   whipped topping,
   thawed

Put the egg yolks, vinegar, and sugar in a saucepan. Bring to a boil and cook over low heat, stirring constantly, until mixture is like custard. Remove from heat, pour into a bowl, and cool thoroughly.

Add gumdrops, marshmallows, pineapple, maraschino cherries, and nuts to the cooled custard, blending well. Fold in the whipped topping. Pour into two metal ice cube trays from which sections have been removed. Freeze overnight.

Before serving, thaw slightly in warm water to remove salad from trays. Slice and place on lettuce or greens on plates. Serves 10 to 12.

LAST-MINUTE SALAD
Vern

This sweet salad is especially good at a potluck or buffet where a number of dishes are being served.

1 can (21 oz.) peach pie
   filling
1 can (21 oz.) apricot pie
   filling
1 can (20 oz.) crushed
   pineapple, drained

2 or 3 bananas, peeled and
   sliced
Fresh seasonal fruit
Marshmallows (optional)

In a large bowl, combine peach pie filling, apricot pie filling, pineapple, and bananas; mix gently. Add any other sliced seasonal fruit—strawberries, fresh peaches, or any berries. Add a few marshmallows, if desired. Chill. Serves 10 to 12, depending on amount of fruit.

VERSATILE SALAD
Vern

1 pkg. (3 oz.) gelatin
(flavor depends on fruit)
1 pt. cottage cheese
1 can (20 oz.) crushed
pineapple
1 can (20 oz.) fruit (see
directions)

½ cup chopped pecans
1 container (8 oz.) frozen
whipped topping,
thawed

With lime gelatin, use pears and pineapple. With orange gelatin, use apricots and pineapple. With strawberry or raspberry gelatin, use peaches and pineapple. With grape gelatin, use bananas and nuts.

In a large bowl, sprinkle dry gelatin over the cottage cheese. Mix well. Let stand for 30 minutes. Fold in the fruit with juices, pecans, and whipped topping. Refrigerate. Serves 8 generously.

CHERRY SUPREME SALAD
Vern

1 pkg. (3 oz.) raspberry-
flavored gelatin
2 cups water, boiling
1 can (20 oz.) cherry pie
filling, undrained
1 pkg. (3 oz.) lemon-fla-
vored gelatin
1 pkg. (3 oz.) cream
cheese, softened

⅓ cup mayonnaise
1 cup undrained crushed
pineapple
1 container (8 oz.) frozen
whipped topping,
thawed
1 cup miniature marshmal-
lows
Chopped nuts (for garnish)

In a bowl, dissolve the raspberry-flavored gelatin in 1 cup boiling water. Stir in the cherry pie filling. Pour into a 9-inch square dish, and set to firm in the refrigerator.

In a bowl, dissolve the lemon-flavored gelatin in 1 cup of boiling water. Chill until slightly congealed. In another bowl, beat the cream cheese and mayonnaise together, then stir in the undrained pineapple. Fold in the whipped topping. Fold mixture into the slightly congealed lemon-flavored gelatin and stir in marshmallows. Spread on top of congealed cherry gelatin mixture. Sprinkle the top with chopped nuts. Serves 9.

LEMON FRUIT SALAD
Vern

This is one of my most requested recipes. It is versatile, and other fruits in season, such as strawberries, may be added.

1 can (11 oz.) mandarin
    oranges, well drained
1 can (8 oz.) pineapple
    tidbits, well drained
1 can (8½ oz.) fruit
    cocktail, undrained
1 banana, sliced
Strawberries (or other
    fruit), as desired

1 pkg. (3 oz.) lemon-
    flavored instant pudding
    mix
1 container (8 oz.) frozen
    whipped topping,
    thawed

In a large bowl, combine oranges, pineapple tidbits, fruit cocktail, banana, strawberries, and other fruits of choice. Sprinkle on the package of dry instant lemon pudding mix. Let set for 15 minutes, gently stirring occasionally. Fold in the whipped topping. Chill. Serves 10 to 12.

CRANBERRY CANDLE SALAD
Vern

1 pkg. (3 oz.) red cherry or
raspberry-flavored
gelatin
1 cup water, boiling
½ cup mayonnaise
1 apple, diced

2 bananas, sliced
1 can (1 lb.) whole
cranberry sauce
1 tbsp. lemon juice
¼ tsp. salt
¼ cup chopped walnuts

Prepare 6 empty, clean, frozen-juice cans (6-oz. size) to use as molds.

In a mixing bowl, prepare gelatin according to package directions, using 1 cup boiling water. Chill until partially congealed. In another bowl, combine mayonnaise, diced apple, bananas, whole cranberry sauce, lemon juice, salt, and walnuts. Fold cranberry mixture into partially congealed gelatin. Spoon gelatin mixture into the juice cans for a festive, red candle appearance. Chill in refrigerator until firm.

To serve, unmold red candles onto lettuce leaves on plates or a serving platter. Serves 6.

SPINACH SALAD
Vern

1 lb. fresh spinach
1 container (12 oz.)
cottage cheese
1 cup chopped pecans
1 cup (8 oz.) sour cream

½ cup sugar
3 tbsp. vinegar
1½ tsp. dry mustard
2 tsp. horseradish
½ tsp. salt

Wash spinach well. Pat dry on a tea towel or use paper toweling. Chill until crisp. Rinse the cottage cheese; drain thoroughly.

Tear spinach into bite-size pieces, and place in a bowl. Add cottage cheese and pecans to the spinach; mix lightly. In a small bowl, combine sour cream, sugar, vinegar, mustard, horseradish, and salt. Mix well. Combine the sour cream and spinach mixtures just before serving. Serves 6 to 8.

Note: The salad and dressing can be prepared ahead of time, stored separately, and tossed right before serving.

LUNCHEON SEAFOOD SALAD
Vern

A more expensive salad to make than most, this one is fancy enough for special guests.

1 pkg. (16 oz.) macaroni
(plain or fancy)
2 cans (4¼ oz. each)
medium-size shrimp,
drained
2 cans (6½ oz. each) tuna
fish (chunk light or
albacore packed in
water), drained
1 can (6 oz.) crabmeat,
drained

12 eggs, hard-cooked,
peeled, and chopped
1 cup diced celery
1 jar (4 oz.) sliced red
pimientos, chopped
1½ tsp. salt (or to taste)
½ pt. whipping cream
2 cups mayonnaise

Cook macaroni according to package directions. Rinse, drain, place in a bowl, and cool.

In a large bowl, combine shrimp, tuna fish, crabmeat, chopped hard-cooked eggs, celery, pimientos, and salt; mix well. In another bowl, add the whipping cream to the mayonnaise and blend well. Combine the macaroni, seafood mixture, and dressing; stir until dressing and all ingredients are well mixed. Chill in the refrigerator for at least 1 hour before serving. However, this salad tastes even better if prepared a day ahead of time. Serves 12 to 16 generously.

FROG EYE SALAD
Vern

This recipe will have your guests guessing! It is both unusual and delicious!

1 box (15 oz.) Soup Macs
or tiny pasta
1 cup sugar
3 eggs, lightly beaten
¾ cup pineapple juice
(drained from crushed
pineapple)
½ tsp. salt
1 can (8¼ oz.) crushed
pineapple, drained
(reserve liquid)

2 cans (11 oz. each)
mandarin oranges,
drained
1 can (8¼ oz.) pineapple
tidbits, drained (reserve
liquid)
1 pkg. (16 oz.) miniature
marshmallows
1 container (16 oz.) frozen
whipped topping,
thawed

Cook pasta according to package directions; rinse, drain, place in a large bowl, and chill.

In a saucepan, combine sugar, eggs, ¾ cup pineapple juice, and salt; mix well. Cook over low heat, stirring constantly, until thickened. Pour over the chilled pasta and toss gently to mix well. Fold in crushed pineapple, mandarin oranges, pineapple tidbits, marshmallows, and whipped topping. Refrigerate for 2 hours or overnight. Serves 12.

Note: This dish may be frozen. It keeps well in the freezer. Leftover juices may be saved and used to set gelatins or added to cold drinks in hot weather.

CHILLED PINEAPPLE SALAD
Vern

8 slices canned pineapple
(1 for each serving)
½ cup bottled French
dressing
1 pkg. (8 oz.) cream
cheese, softened
1 cup chopped walnuts or
pecans or 1 cup drained
and chopped maraschino
or mint cherries

Lettuce (for garnish)
⅓ cup whipping cream,
whipped
⅔ cup mayonnaise

Allow a slice of canned pineapple for each serving. In a bowl, baste pineapple slices with a commercial French dressing made with lemon juice. Place each pineapple slice on a bed of lettuce on an individual salad plate. Fill center of each pineapple slice with a marble-size ball made of cream cheese rolled in chopped nutmeats—either walnuts or pecans—or in chopped maraschino cherries or mint cherries. Chill the salads.

When ready to serve, fold the whipped cream into the mayonnaise, blending well. Serve each salad with a dollop of dressing. Serves 8.

SALAD DRESSING
Vern

2 eggs
2 tbsp. sugar
1 tbsp. butter
1 tsp. dry mustard

Pepper to taste
Salt to taste
1 cup cider vinegar

In a small bowl, beat the eggs, then combine the beaten eggs, sugar, butter, mustard, salt, and pepper in the top of a double boiler. Cook over medium heat, gradually adding cider vinegar and stirring occasionally until thick. Allow to cool before using. Makes 1¼ cups dressing.

Note: This dressing can be stored in refrigerator for several weeks.

FROZEN FRUIT FOR BREAKFAST, LUNCH, OR DINNER
Vern

This is a refreshing summer treat! Prepare it the night before. Individual servings are ideal for a bridal shower or a brunch.

1 can (20 oz.) pineapple
chunks, drain (reserve
juice)
Water (as needed)
1¼ cups sugar
1 pkg. (10 oz.) frozen
strawberries

1 can (16 oz.) apricots,
drained
1 can (11 oz.) mandarin
oranges, drained
2 bananas, sliced
Lettuce leaves (to line
plates)

Drain the pineapple chunks and save the juice. Add enough water to the pineapple juice to make 1 cup of liquid. Combine the sugar and the liquid in a medium-size saucepan and cook until the sugar is dissolved. Add frozen strawberries, and stir to thaw. Cool.

Fold in pineapple chunks, apricots, mandarin oranges, and bananas, mixing well. Pour fruit mixture into a large glass bowl for a pretty dish. Freeze. To serve, remove from freezer and allow to become slushy. Serve in cups or glass dishes. Top each serving with a dollop of Popular Topping (recipe follows). Serves 12.

Note: Freeze mixture in a 9 x 13 x 2-inch pan so the fruit can be cut into squares and served on lettuce leaves on individual plates. Remove from freezer about 30 minutes before serving. Any fruit may be substituted.

POPULAR TOPPING FOR FROZEN OR FRESH FRUIT
Vern

1 jar (7 oz.) marshmallow
cream
1 pkg. (8 oz.) cream
cheese, at room
temperature

Red or green maraschino
juice for color, as desired
½ cup coconut (optional)

In a small bowl, combine marshmallow cream, softened cream cheese, juice, and coconut. Mix until smooth. Cover and keep in the refrigerator for use anytime.

Note: Tester Melisa Breheny of Rock Island used crème de menthe for color and omitted the coconut.

Vegetables and Other Side Dishes

SCALLOPED TURNIPS
Sara

Turnips are boiled plain with or without meat, and sometimes mashed like potatoes or stewed like parsnips. They always should be served hot.

3 to 4 cups peeled and
thinly sliced turnips
½ cup chopped onion
1 tbsp. flour
¼ cup butter, chunked

Salt and pepper to taste
1 cup milk
½ cup bread or cracker
crumbs

Alternate layers of turnip slices and chopped onion in a 1-quart baking dish. Use about four times as many turnips as onions. Sprinkle flour between layers. Place chunks of butter and sprinkle salt and pepper, as desired, over each layer of onion.

Heat oven to 350 degrees. Pour milk over the top and sprinkle on bread or cracker crumbs. Bake at 350 degrees until turnips are tender, about 1 hour. Test with a fork for tenderness. Serves 6 to 8.

VEGETABLES
Elizabeth Jane

In the late 1800s and early 1900s, the cooking methods were very different. Vegetables often were overcooked until vitamins were reduced. This entry was included to show how differently we prepare vegetables today.

Use freshly picked vegetables. Soak them, when peeled, in cold water for some time before cooking. If to be boiled, put a little salt in the water. Cook steadily after you put them on. Test for tenderness, but do not cook to a mushy stage. Drain well and serve hot.

CABBAGE
Elizabeth Jane

This recipe also shows historical differences in cooking methods.

In preparing the various dishes from this excellent vegetable, care should be taken in the choice of heads. For boiling or for hot coleslaws, loose heads may be used, but for slicing and eating raw with the different kinds of dressing, a white, firm head should be selected. Many who like cabbage will not cook it because of the odor which it exudes. To prevent odor, put a piece of charcoal tied in a cloth into the pot with the cabbage, and simmer instead of boiling. One medium-size head of cabbage, cooked, serves 6 to 8.

STRING BEANS
Elizabeth Jane

Note the long cooking time in the original recipe.

2 qt. fresh beans   **Salt pork**
Water (as needed)

String, snap, wash, and drain 2 quarts of beans. In a saucepan, boil the beans for 15 minutes in enough water to cover them. Drain and cover again with 2 quarts of water. Boil for 1½ hours with salt pork. For shelled beans, boil 1 hour longer. Serves about 10.

Note: Today, we cook the beans for 15 minutes in as little water as possible to preserve vitamins. Season with butter.

WINTER SQUASH
Elizabeth Jane

Winter squash requires more time for cooking than summer squashes.

6 lb. winter squash	**Butter (optional)**
Water (to cover)	**Salt and pepper to taste**

Wash squash, cut into medium-sized pieces, pare, and remove seeds. In a kettle, cover with water and boil until tender, about ½ hour. Drain as dry as possible, and let the squash stand a few minutes on the top of the stove so that all the water may evaporate. Mash the squash.

Heat oven to 350 degrees. Place mashed squash in a 1 to 1½-quart casserole. Season with butter, salt, and pepper, as desired. Bake, uncovered, at 350 degrees for about 1 hour. Makes 8 to 10 servings.

BOILED DANDELIONS
Jessie

My mother, Jessie, was the only one who liked this dish, but she sent us out to gather young dandelions, and fixed it for herself! Use the tender shoots of the dandelions. After blossoming, they become bitter and stringy. Collect more than 1 quart of dandelions to serve 1 person.

1 qt. dandelion stems	**1 tbsp. butter**
Water (to cover)	**Salt and pepper to taste**
1 tsp. salt	

EGG SAUCE:

1 tbsp. butter or	**⅛ tsp. pepper**
margarine	**1 cup milk**
1 tbsp. flour	**¼ cup chopped onions**
¼ tsp. salt	**2 hard-cooked eggs, diced**

Cut off the roots and pick over the dandelions carefully, discarding imperfect stems. Wash well several times. Put them in a saucepan, cover with water, and add a teaspoon of salt. Boil 15 minutes (Jessie boiled them for 1 hour). When done, drain and chop fine. Place dandelions in a frying pan and add butter and salt and pepper to taste. Stir until thoroughly heated.

In a small saucepan, heat margarine over low heat until melted. Blend in flour, salt, and pepper. Cook over low heat, stirring constantly, until smooth and bubbly. Remove from heat. Stir in milk. Return to heat and bring to boiling, stirring constantly. Boil gently and stir for 1 minute. Add the chopped onions and hard-cooked eggs. If preferred, onions may be sautéed first for more tender texture. Pour over dandelion greens and serve. Serves 1 person.

Note: In the early days, Jessie would have used bacon fat instead of butter.

SWEET POTATOES
IN BROWN SUGAR SYRUP
Lavina

8 to 10 sweet potatoes	**1 tsp. salt**
1 cup firmly packed brown sugar	**½ cup butter or margarine**

Scrub and bake the sweet potatoes until tender. Cool and peel. Heat oven to 350 degrees. Grease a 1-quart casserole. Place whole potatoes in the casserole, sprinkle with brown sugar and salt, and dot with butter. Bake, uncovered, for 30 minutes, or until done. Makes 8 to 10 servings.

FRIED POTATOES AND ONIONS
Lavina

1 medium onion, diced
1 red or green pepper,
    diced (optional)
¼ cup butter, melted

4 or 5 medium potatoes,
    sliced
Salt and pepper to taste

In a skillet, sauté onion and pepper in melted butter. Add sliced potatoes and fry, turning often, until golden brown. Season with salt and pepper. Serves 4 or 5.

Note: Fresh potatoes, leftover baked potatoes, or frozen hash browns are tasty prepared this way.

BROCCOLI AND CORN SCALLOP
Vern

This recipe may be prepared ahead and served with a variety of vegetable dishes, for example, at a potluck meal or a large family dinner.

1 pkg. (10 oz.) frozen
    chopped broccoli
1 small onion, chopped
½ cup cracker crumbs
1 egg, beaten

1 can (16 oz.) cream-style
    corn
1 cup shredded cheddar
    cheese

Cook broccoli according to package directions; drain and place in a small bowl. Mix onion with the broccoli and set aside. In another small bowl, mix the cracker crumbs with the beaten egg.

Heat oven to 350 degrees. Place a layer of corn in a greased 11 x 7-inch baking dish. Top with a layer of broccoli, then a layer of crumbs. Repeat and top with grated cheese, as desired. Bake at 350 degrees for 30 minutes. Makes 6 servings.

GOLDEN CARROTS
Vern

Everyone loves carrots prepared this way!

12 carrots, peeled and
  sliced
1 onion, chopped
2 tbsp. butter or mar-
  garine

1⅓ cups milk
Salt and pepper to taste
½ lb. American cheese,
  cubed
½ cup bread crumbs

In a saucepan, cook carrots in a small amount of water, until tender but crisp, about 10 minutes. Drain. In another saucepan, sauté
the onion in margarine. Add the milk, salt, and pepper; mix well.
Cook over low heat until hot, but do not boil.

Heat oven to 325 degrees. In a buttered 1½-quart casserole, layer
the carrots and pieces of cheese. Pour the hot milk mixture over all.
Top with bread crumbs. Bake, covered, for 45 minutes. Serves 8.

ASPARAGUS OR SPINACH SOUFFLE
Vern

*This makes a nice, light accompaniment to a meal at which
other dishes are more colorful.*

4 eggs, separated
1 can (10¾ oz.) condensed
  asparagus or spinach
  soup

¾ cup grated American or
  cheddar cheese

In a bowl, beat egg yolks until light and lemon colored. Set aside.
In the top of a double boiler, heat the soup with the cheese until
cheese is melted and smooth. Remove from heat and add a little of
the hot mixture to the egg yolks. Mix well, then stir into the remaining soup-cheese mixture.

In a bowl, beat egg whites until stiff. Carefully fold stiffly beaten egg whites into the soup mixture. Heat oven to 325 degrees. Pour mixture into an ungreased 1½-quart casserole. Place the casserole into a shallow pan and place in oven. Carefully pour water into the shallow pan to a depth of about 1 inch. Bake at 325 degrees for 1 hour. Serve at once. Serves 4.

BAKED CAULIFLOWER
Vern

1 large head cauliflower	2 tsp. dry mustard
1 cup water	1 cup cheddar or American
½ tsp. salt	cheese, grated
½ cup mayonnaise	

Clean, core, and chop cauliflower into florets. In a saucepan or small kettle, bring water to boiling; add salt. Add cauliflower to boiling water. When boiling again, partially cover and cook cauliflower for 10 minutes. Remove from heat and drain well.

Heat oven to 350 degrees. In a small bowl, combine mayonnaise and mustard; mix well. Place the cauliflower in a greased 1-quart casserole and cover with the mayonnaise-mustard mixture. Top with grated cheese. Bake, uncovered, at 350 degrees until mixture bubbles, about 20 minutes. Serves 4.

DILLY GREEN BEANS
Vern

1½ lb. fresh green beans	¾ cup sour cream
2 tbsp. margarine	1 tsp. dill weed
2 tbsp. chopped chives	

In a saucepan or kettle, cook beans in salted water to cover until tender-crisp. Drain.

In a skillet or saucepan, melt the margarine, then lightly sauté the chives. Add sour cream and dill weed, mix well, and heat through, but do not boil. Pour over beans. Serves 4.

SCALLOPED APPLES
Vern

Serve this as a side dish with ham or in addition to vegetables. I always double this recipe.

4 medium-size apples,
  peeled, cored, and sliced
½ cup sugar
¼ tsp. ground cloves

¼ tsp. ground cinnamon
2 cups fresh bread cubes
½ cup butter, melted

Heat oven to 350 degrees. Place peeled and sliced apples into a bowl. Sprinkle with sugar, cloves, and cinnamon. In a skillet, toss fresh bread cubes in melted butter.

Grease an 8 x 8-inch baking pan (or a 9 x 13-inch baking pan for a double recipe). Layer half the apples, then the bread cubes. Repeat. Bake, uncovered, at 350 degrees for 1 hour. Serves 4.

CELERY BAKE
Vern

This is a very attractive dish with colorful garnishes.

1 cup water
½ tsp. salt
5 cups celery, cut into
  bite-size pieces
1 can (10¾ oz.) cream of
  chicken soup
1 can (6 oz.) sliced water
  chestnuts, drained

1 jar (2 oz.) pimientos,
  drained and chopped
Slivered almonds (for
  topping)
Fresh parsley and cherry
  tomatoes (for garnishes)

Heat oven to 350 degrees. In a saucepan, bring water to boiling; add salt and celery. Cover and bring to boiling; then cook for 5 minutes. Drain. Combine cooked celery with soup, water chestnuts, and pimientos. Place mixture in a greased 1-quart casserole. Top with slivered almonds. Bake, uncovered, for 30 to 45 minutes. Garnish with fresh parsley and/or cherry tomatoes. Serves 4.

SPINACH CASSEROLE
Vern

1 cup uncooked rice
2 pkg. (10 oz. each) frozen
  chopped spinach,
  thawed and well-drained
1 egg, beaten
2 tbsp. onion flakes
1 tsp. Worcestershire
  sauce

1 tsp. salt
1 cup milk
2 tbsp. butter, melted
½ cup shredded sharp
  cheddar cheese
Dash paprika

Heat oven to 325 degrees. Grease a 2-quart casserole or coat with a nonstick vegetable spray.

In a saucepan, cook the rice according according to package directions; drain. Combine cooked rice and spinach in a large bowl. In a small bowl or large measuring cup, mix the beaten egg, onion flakes, Worcestershire sauce, salt, and milk. Stir into the rice-spinach mixture.

Pour mixture into the prepared 2-quart casserole. Top with melted butter and shredded cheese. Sprinkle with paprika. Bake, uncovered, at 325 degrees, for 40 minutes. Serves 6 to 8.

ZUCCHINI DISH
Vern

6 cups sliced zucchini
¼ cup chopped onion
Water (as needed)
1 tsp. salt
1 can (10¾ oz.) cream of
  chicken soup
1 cup sour cream

1 cup finely shredded
  carrots
1 pkg. (8 oz.) seasoned
  herb stuffing mix
½ cup butter or margarine,
  melted

Preheat oven to 350 degrees. In a covered saucepan or kettle, cook zucchini and onion in boiling salted water for 5 minutes. Drain.

In a bowl, combine soup and sour cream; mix well. Stir in carrots. Fold in the zucchini and onions. In another bowl, combine the stuffing mix with melted butter or margarine, mixing well. Spread half the stuffing mix in the bottom of a lightly greased 9 x 13 x 2-inch baking dish. Spoon the vegetable mixture on top. Sprinkle remaining stuffing over the vegetables. Bake, uncovered, at 350 degrees for 30 minutes. Serves 4 to 6.

FANCY SQUASH DISH

Vern

2 lb. butternut squash	1 can (10¾ oz.) cream of
1 cup water	mushroom soup
Salt to taste	1 cup sour cream
½ cup butter or mar-	1 can (4 oz.) water chest-
garine, melted	nuts, drained and sliced
1 can (10¾ oz.) cream of	1 pkg. (4 oz.) seasoned
chicken soup	dressing mix

To prepare the squash, cut squash into pieces, pare, and remove fibers and seeds. To cook the squash, heat 1 cup of water in a saucepan. When boiling, add salt and squash, cover, and cook until tender, about 15 to 20 minutes. Drain well and mash.

Heat oven to 325 degrees. Grease a 9 x 13 x 2-inch baking dish. In a mixing bowl, combine ¼ cup of the butter, cream of chicken soup, cream of mushroom soup, sour cream, and water chestnuts with the mashed squash.

Line the bottom of the baking dish with the seasoned dressing mix. Spread squash mixture over the dressing mix. Drizzle remaining ¼ cup butter on top. Bake, uncovered, at 325 degrees for 40 minutes. Serves 4.

FANCY POTATO BAKE
Vern

1 pkg. (32 oz.) frozen hash
  brown potatoes
1 can (10¾ oz.) cream of
  chicken soup
1 stick margarine, melted
2 tbsp. onion flakes

1 cup sour cream
2 cups grated American
  cheese
Salt and pepper to taste
1 cup buttered cracker
  crumbs (optional)

Heat oven to 350 degrees. Butter a 9 x 13 x 2-inch baking dish. Thaw the frozen hash brown potatoes for easy mixing. In a large mixing bowl, combine potatoes, cream of chicken soup, melted margarine, onion flakes, sour cream, grated cheese, salt, and pepper. Blend well and pour into prepared baking dish. Sprinkle buttered cracker crumbs on top, if desired. Bake, uncovered, at 350 degrees for 1 hour. Serves 8 to 10.

PARTY TIME POTATOES
Vern

1 pkg. (8 oz.) cream
  cheese, softened
1 cup sour cream
10 potatoes, pared and
  chopped
2½ cups water

½ tsp. salt
Pepper to taste
½ cup grated American or
  colby cheese (optional)
1 tbsp. butter (optional)

Heat oven to 350 degrees. Grease a 2-quart casserole or 9 x 13 x 2-inch baking dish. In a small bowl, combine the cream cheese and sour cream and mix well. Set aside.

Put potatoes in a saucepan with enough water to cover, about 2½ cups. Add salt and cover. Bring to boiling, and cook until potatoes are tender, about 20 to 25 minutes. Drain and mash the potatoes.

In a mixing bowl, stir cream cheese mixture into the hot potatoes, add pepper to taste, then spread in prepared baking dish. Top with grated cheese and dot with butter, if desired. Bake, uncovered, at 350 degrees for about 1 hour, until browned. Serves 10.

SPECIAL POTATOES
Vern

4 baking potatoes
3 tbsp. butter, melted
½ cup shredded sharp
  cheddar cheese

½ cup half-and-half cream
Salt to taste
Pepper to taste

Heat oven to 425 degrees. Clean, pare, and cut potatoes into strips as you would for french fries. Place potatoes in a single layer in a lightly greased 8 x 8-inch casserole, cover with cheese, and drizzle with melted butter. Pour half-and-half cream over the top, and sprinkle with salt and pepper. Cover and bake for 50 minutes. Serves 4.

POTATO WEDGES
Vern

4 large potatoes
1 cup water
Salt to taste

4 tbsp. butter or
  margarine, melted
Pepper to taste

Clean and peel potatoes, then cut in half lengthwise. Slice each half in thirds lengthwise.

In a saucepan, bring water to boiling. Add salt, as desired, and potato wedges. When boiling again, cook the wedges, uncovered, for 3 minutes. Drain and pat dry with paper towels. Heat oven to 450 degrees. Butter a baking dish large enough to lay the potatoes side by side, but not layered. Drizzle melted butter over the top. Sprinkle with pepper, as desired. Bake, uncovered, at 450 degrees for 15 minutes. Turn potatoes over and bake another 15 minutes. Serves 3 or 4.

Cakes and Frostings

CHRISTMAS CAKE
Elizabeth Jane

1 lb. sugar
½ lb. butter
4 eggs
2½ cups flour
2 tsp. baking powder
1 tsp. salt
1 lb. glazed cherries and
  pineapple

1 lb. mixed citrus peel
1 lb. raisins
1 cup wine or pineapple
  juice
1 tsp. vanilla
½ lb. almonds

Line two loaf pans, 9 x 5 x 3 inches, with aluminum foil. Grease the foiled pans. Heat oven to 250 degrees.

Cream sugar and butter. Add eggs; mix well. Measure flour and then sift with baking powder and salt. Coat the fruit and peel well with some of the flour. Add wine or pineapple juice, vanilla, and remaining flour to creamed mixture, blending well. Stir in fruit and nuts. Pour batter into prepared pans. Bake at 250 degrees for 2 to 3 hours. Serves 12 to 15.

WEDDING CAKE
Lavina

This wedding cake recipe comes down through the generations. It now is a very expensive cake to make, but historically, it was used for a wedding. In earlier times, candied fruit was prepared by putting fruit on a screen and leaving it in the sun until it became candied.

1½ lb. butter
3½ cups sugar
18 eggs, separated
1 tsp. lemon extract
½ pt. brandy
2 whole nutmeg, grated
  fresh
2 tsp. mace
7½ cups sifted flour
4 lb. raisins

2 lb. currants
1 lb. candied cherries
1 lb. candied pineapple
1 lb. candied mixed citrus
  peel
1 lb. candied citron
1 lb. almonds, chopped
1 tsp. soda dissolved in 1
  tbsp. water

Use three square pans for tiers: 8 x 8 inches, 6 x 6 inches, and 4 x 4 inches. Enough batter is left over for another 8 x 8-inch pan. Another option is to use five headcheese pans, if available. These are loaves 4¼ x 8 x 3½ inches deep. Cut strips of brown paper as wide as the pans and line the pans, layered three strips deep on sides and six strips in thickness on the bottom, to keep the batter from burning before cakes are done. Grease the strips.

In a large mixing bowl, soften butter and add sugar, working until the mixture is creamy. Separate egg yolks and whites. Beat egg yolks and add them to the creamed mixture. Beat again. In a separate bowl, beat egg whites to a stiff froth and fold into creamed mixture. Stir lemon extract into brandy and add to the mixture. Add nutmeg and mace to flour, and sift over the fruit. Stir in fruit, then nuts, and finally soda dissolved in 1 tablespoon water. Mix well. Pour batter into prepared pans.

Heat oven to 325 degrees. Bake loaf cakes for 2½ to 3 hours; tube cakes 3½ to 4 hours; 2 hours for the large tier; 1½ hours for the middle-size tier; and 1 hour for the small tier. Test for doneness with a toothpick by inserting until it can be removed without batter. Remove from pans and allow to cool on racks. Serves 90.

ANGEL CAKE
Lavina

Lavina's original recipe included no oven temperatures and no explicit measurements; I have added these based on my own use of the recipe. She tested for temperature by putting her hand inside the oven.

1 cup flour	**¼ tsp. salt**
12 large eggs, separated	**1 scant cup white sugar**
1½ tsp. cream of tartar	**1 tsp. vanilla**

Use an angel food cake pan, but do not grease it. The batter must stick to the sides to rise properly.

In one bowl, measure the flour and sift three times. In another mixing bowl, separate the eggs, setting aside the yolks for another use. Beat the whites with a wire whisk, adding the cream of tartar and salt.

Add the scant cup of sugar to this mixture a little at a time, then add the vanilla. Sift the flour on top, and fold into the meringue.

Heat oven to 375 degrees. Pour batter into angel food cake pan and bake for 30 to 35 minutes, or until top springs back lightly when touched. Cool upside down in the pan.

Note: Leftover egg yolks may be used to make the following sponge cake or to make salad dressing.

BAKE DAY CAKE
Lavina

On bake day, Grandma prepared a sponge (yeast, sugar, water, and a small amount of flour), covered it with a small blanket or rug, and set it behind the stove overnight. In the morning, she used a cup of the bubbly mixture to start her cake. My mother and I both made it.

1 cake or pkg. active dry yeast	1 tsp. salt
¼ cup warm water	1 tsp. soda
1 cup sugar	1 tsp. nutmeg
¼ cup butter	1 tsp. cinnamon
2 eggs	½ cup warm coffee
4 tbsp. molasses	½ cup raisins
1 cup flour	½ cup chopped black walnuts

Grease and flour a 9 x 13 x 2-inch pan. Heat oven to 350 degrees. Soften yeast in ¼ cup warm water. Cream sugar and butter together, then add eggs and beat well. Add molasses and yeast mixture, mixing well.

Sift flour with salt, soda, nutmeg, and cinnamon. Add flour mixture alternately to creamed mixture with warm coffee. Stir in raisins and walnuts. Pour batter into prepared pan. Bake at 350 degrees for 40 minutes. Let cool. Frost with Butter Cream Coffee Frosting for Bake Day Cake (recipe follows).

Note: This cake is moist and keeps a long time.

BUTTER CREAM COFFEE FROSTING FOR BAKE DAY CAKE

¼ cup butter or margarine
⅛ tsp. salt
1 tbsp. flour

2 cups powdered sugar
2 to 3 tbsp. hot coffee

Cream butter or margarine with the salt. Blend flour into powdered sugar and add to the creamed mixture, alternating with hot coffee. Stir until creamy. If frosting is too stiff, add small amounts of coffee until it is of spreading consistency. Spread frosting on Bake Day Cake.

BROWN SUGAR DEVIL'S FOOD CAKE
Lavina

1 cup brown sugar
½ cup cocoa
1 cup milk
1 cup white sugar
½ cup butter

2 eggs, separated
1 tsp. baking soda
1 cup hot water
2 cups flour
2 egg whites, beaten

Grease and lightly flour a 9 x 13 x 2-inch cake pan, or two 8 or 9 x ½-inch layer pans.

In a saucepan, combine brown sugar, cocoa, and milk; bring to a boil, and cook until thick. Set aside. In a large bowl, cream white sugar, butter, and egg yolks. Dissolve baking soda in 1 cup hot water. Immediately add the soda water and thickened brown sugar mixture to the creamed mixture. Stir in flour, blending well.

Heat oven to 350 degrees. Beat egg whites until stiff, and fold into batter. Pour batter into prepared pan(s) and bake at 350 degrees for about 35 minutes, or until done. Test for doneness by inserting a toothpick in the center of the cake until it can be removed clean. When cooled, frost with Brown Sugar Frosting (recipe follows).

BROWN SUGAR FROSTING

2 cups brown sugar
½ cup cream or half-
and-half

1 tbsp. butter
1 tbsp. vanilla

In a saucepan, combine ingredients, except for vanilla, and bring to a boil like fudge. Use a candy thermometer to test for soft-ball stage, or drop a small amount of the mixture into a glass of cold water until it forms a soft ball between two fingers. Remove from heat and add vanilla. Beat until smooth. Allow frosting to cool before spreading on cake. Frosts a 9 x 13 x 2-inch cake generously.

GINGERBREAD
Lavina

Early cooks used bacon grease for flavor. Today's cooks, more aware of health and nutrition, use margarine or vegetable oil.

½ cup hot water
½ cup molasses
½ cup bacon grease
1 egg, beaten
1½ cups flour

½ tsp. baking soda
½ cup sugar
¼ tsp. salt
1 tsp. cinnamon
1 tsp. ginger

In a small bowl, mix hot water and molasses. Add fat, then beaten egg. In a larger bowl, mix dry ingredients. Add liquid mixture and stir hard.

Heat oven to 325 degrees. Pour batter into a greased 8 x 8-inch square pan, and bake until done, about 50 minutes, until a toothpick inserted in center comes out clean. Makes 9 servings.

HICKORY NUT CAKE
Jessie

Before the days of electric mixers, cooks used a warm hand as a mixing tool to melt shortening and any remaining sugar granules.

3 cups flour
5 tsp. baking powder
¼ tsp. salt
⅔ cup butter
2 cups sugar

1¼ cups water
4 egg whites
1 tsp. vanilla
1 cup chopped hickory
  nutmeats

Grease and flour two 9-inch layer pans. Heat oven to 350 degrees.

In a mixing bowl, sift flour with 4 teaspoons baking powder and salt. In another bowl, cream butter and sugar in a bowl until the granulation has dissolved. Add flour mixture to creamed ingredients, alternating with water.

With a whisk or electric mixer, whip egg whites with remaining teaspoon baking powder until peaks form. Fold beaten egg whites into batter; then fold in vanilla and nuts. Pour batter into prepared pans. Bake at 350 degrees until done, about 20 to 25 minutes. To test for doneness, insert a toothpick in center of cakes until it comes out clean. Frost with Jessie's Seven-Minute Frosting (recipe follows). Serves 12 to 16.

JESSIE'S SEVEN-MINUTE FROSTING

1 cup sugar
¼ tsp. salt
¼ tsp. cream of tartar

2 egg whites, unbeaten
2 tbsp. water
1 tsp. vanilla

Combine all ingredients except vanilla in top of a double boiler. Place over boiling water. Using an electric hand mixer, beat until stiff peaks form, or exactly 7 minutes. Remove from heat, fold in vanilla, and spread on cooled cake.

SOUR CREAM CHOCOLATE CAKE
Jessie

This cake is better when made with thick sour cream, but I have used commercial sour cream as well.

1¾ cups flour
1¼ cups sugar
4 tbsp. cocoa
2 eggs
1½ cups sour cream

1 tbsp. butter
1 tsp. vanilla
2 tsp. baking soda
¼ cup hot water

Grease and flour a 9 x 13-inch pan. Heat oven to 350 degrees.
In a mixing bowl, sift flour, sugar, and cocoa together until well blended. Set aside. In another bowl, beat eggs, sour cream, and butter until light. Add vanilla and flour mixture, mixing well. In a small cup, dissolve baking soda in hot water and stir into batter, blending well. Pour batter into prepared pan. Bake at 350 degrees for 30 minutes, or until cake tests done when toothpick inserted in center comes out clean. Serves 12.

EGGLESS MILKLESS BUTTERLESS CAKE
Jessie

A Depression Era cake with a wonderful aroma, this cake has the texture of moist bar cookies. It's an inexpensive cake that can serve many.

¾ cup raisins
1½ cups water
1 cup packed brown sugar
½ cup shortening
2¼ cups flour
2 tsp. baking powder
¼ tsp. baking soda
¾ tsp. allspice
½ tsp. cloves

½ tsp. cinnamon
½ tsp. salt (optional)
½ cup chopped nuts
  (optional)
Confectioners' sugar
  (optional)
Whipped topping or ice
  cream

Grease and flour a 9 x 13 x 2-inch pan for a cake, or a jelly-roll pan for cookie bars. Heat oven to 350 degrees.

In a large measuring cup or small bowl, combine raisins and hot water. Let stand for 20 minutes. In a large bowl, cream brown sugar and shortening. In another bowl, sift flour, baking powder, baking soda, spices, and salt. Add flour mixture to creamed mixture and blend well, adding the liquid from the raisins. Add remaining raisin mixture and nuts. Mix well. Pour batter into prepared pan. Bake at 350 degrees for 45 minutes in 9 x 13-inch pan, and for 30 minutes if using jelly-roll pan.

When slightly cooled, sprinkle cake with confectioners' sugar, or this cake is also good served with a commercial whipped topping or ice cream. Serves 12-15.

POOR MAN'S CAKE
Jessie

This is a recipe that also was used frequently during the Depression years. This recipe is interesting because it includes basic ingredients that were available to most early cooks and it offers a historical perspective on frugality.

2 cups flour
¼ cup cocoa
1 tsp. baking powder
1 tsp. baking soda

1 tsp. salt
1 cup white sugar
1 cup mayonnaise or salad dressing

Grease a 9 x 13 x 2-inch pan. Heat oven to 350 degrees. In a large mixing bowl, sift together the flour, cocoa, baking powder, baking soda, and salt. In another bowl, blend sugar and mayonnaise. Add to the flour mixture and beat well. Pour into prepared pan. Bake at 350 degrees for 30 minutes. This cake needs no frosting and is especially good served warm. Serves 12.

QUICK AND EASY TWO EGG CAKE
Vern

Easy to mix and delicious served warm, this cake can also be served unfrosted, with fruit, or as strawberry shortcake.

2 cups sifted cake flour
2½ tsp. baking powder
½ tsp. salt
1⅓ cups sugar
½ cup soft shortening

⅔ cup milk
1 tsp. vanilla
2 eggs
¼ cup milk

Grease and flour a 9 x 13 x 2-inch pan. Heat oven to 350 degrees. Combine first seven ingredients in a large bowl of electric mixer. Beat at medium speed for 2 minutes. Add eggs and ¼ cup milk, then beat again until light and fluffy. Pour batter into prepared pan. Bake at 350 degrees for 25 to 30 minutes until cake tests done when toothpick inserted in center comes out clean. This cake is best eaten the day it's made. Serves 12.

SPRINGTIME MERINGUE CAKE
Vern

This is a spectacular, two-layer cake for a special occasion.

1 pkg. (2-layer size) yellow
cake mix
1 cup orange juice
4 egg yolks
1½ tsp. grated orange peel
4 egg whites

¼ tsp. cream of tartar
1 cup sugar
2 cups sliced strawberries
2 tbsp. sugar
1 cup whipping cream

Grease generously two 9 x 1½-inch round cake pans clear to the tops of the rims. Line each with brown paper and grease again. Heat oven to 350 degrees.

In the large bowl of an electric mixer, combine the first four ingredients and beat for 4 minutes at medium speed. Pour batter into prepared pans.

Place egg whites in medium-size bowl of electric mixer. Add cream of tartar and beat until soft peaks form. Slowly add 1 cup of sugar, then beat until stiff peaks form. Divide meringue evenly, spreading half over the batter in each of the pans. Bake at 350 degrees for 35 minutes. Remove from pans, placing the cakes meringue side up on racks. Allow to cool slightly.

Rinse, thoroughly drain, and hull strawberries. Mash enough strawberries to make ½ cup and stir in 2 tablespoons sugar. Reserve remaining berries to slice and use between the layers and to decorate the top. In a medium-size bowl, whip the cream until stiff. Fold in mashed strawberries.

To assemble: Place the first layer of the cake on a cake plate, meringue side up. Spread ⅔ of the whipped cream mixture over the first layer. Slice enough of the reserved berries to spread evenly over the whipped cream mixture. Add the second cake layer, meringue side up. Spread with remaining whipped cream mixture, and decorate with remaining berries. Store in the refrigerator until ready to serve. Serves 12 to 15.

SNOW-TOPPED CHOCOLATE CARAMEL CAKE
Vern

1 pkg. (18¼ oz.) German
  chocolate cake mix
1 pkg. (14 oz.) caramels
¾ cup butter or margarine
½ cup evaporated milk
1 cup chocolate chips

1 cup chopped pecans
Confectioners' sugar,
  sifted
Ice cream or whipped
  cream

Grease and flour a 9 x 13 x 2-inch pan. Heat oven to 350 degrees.

Mix the cake batter according to package directions. Pour half the batter into prepared pan, and bake for 15 minutes. Reserve the remaining half of batter.

Combine caramels, butter, and evaporated milk in a heavy saucepan over low heat, stirring until candies are melted and mixture is blended. Pour over partly baked cake. Sprinkle with chocolate chips and nuts. Carefully spread reserved batter over the top. Return cake to oven and bake at 350 degrees for 20 minutes more.

Remove cake from oven and sprinkle sifted confectioners' sugar over the top. Allow to cool. Cut in squares, and serve with ice cream or whipped cream. Serves 12 to 16.

CHOCOL-OAT CAKE
Vern

This has been a favorite cake for more than twenty years.

1¼ cups boiling water	**1 cup brown sugar**
1 cup quick-cooking oats	**2 eggs**
½ cup cocoa	**1⅓ cups flour**
½ cup butter	**1 tsp. soda**
1 cup white sugar	**1 tsp. salt**

BROWN SUGAR TOPPING:

⅔ cup brown sugar	**6 tbsp. butter, softened**
1 cup flaked coconut	**3 tbsp. cocoa**
1 cup chopped nutmeats	**¼ cup milk**

Grease and flour a 9 x 13-inch pan. Heat oven to 350 degrees.

In a medium-size bowl, pour boiling water over quick-cooking oats and cocoa. Let stand 15 minutes. In a large mixing bowl, cream together butter, white sugar, and brown sugar. Add eggs and beat well. In a small bowl, sift together flour, soda, and salt. Add the oats mixture and flour to the creamed mixture, and beat until smooth. Pour batter into prepared pan. Bake at 350 degrees for 35 to 40 minutes.

While cake is baking, combine Brown Sugar Topping ingredients in a saucepan and cook over low heat, stirring until well mixed. When cake tests done with a toothpick inserted near the center, remove from the oven and cover with topping. Return cake to oven and bake for about 10 minutes more, until topping is bubbly. Serves 12 to 16.

WARM APPLE CAKE
WITH BUTTER SAUCE
Vern

2 cups flour
1 cup quick-cooking oats
2 tsp. cinnamon
1 tsp. salt
1 tsp. baking soda
1 cup white sugar
1 cup brown sugar

1¼ cups cooking oil
2 eggs
2 tsp. vanilla
½ tsp. almond extract
3 cups raw, peeled, thinly
  sliced apples
1 cup chopped nuts

Grease a 9 x 13 x 2-inch pan. Heat oven to 350 degrees. In a medium-size bowl, combine flour, oats, cinnamon, salt, and soda. Set aside. In a large bowl, combine sugars, oil, eggs, and flavorings; mix well. Add flour mixture, apples, and nuts to sugar mixture, blending well. Pour batter into prepared pan. Bake at 350 degrees for 1 hour. Serve warm with butter sauce. Serves 12.

BUTTER SAUCE

This sauce is good on any cake, such as the Warm Apple Cake, or chocolate or spice, as a frosting substitute.

1 cup white sugar
½ cup butter

¾ cup heavy cream
½ tsp. vanilla

Place sugar and butter in a saucepan and cook over low heat, stirring until well dissolved. Slowly add the cream, mixing until well blended and heated. Remove sauce from heat and stir in vanilla. Cool slightly before serving.

WINTER WHITE HOLIDAY FRUIT CAKE
Vern

1 lb. butter or margarine
2 cups sugar
6 eggs, separated
3½ cups flour
2 tsp. lemon extract

1 lb. whole pecans
1½ lb. candied red or
   green cherries
¼ lb. candied pineapple
1 lb. white raisins

Grease and flour three 9 x 5 x 3-inch bread pans liberally. Heat oven to 300 degrees.

In a large mixing bowl, cream butter and sugar together until very creamy. Add the egg yolks, 3 cups of flour, and lemon extract; mix well. In a medium-size bowl, combine and lightly flour the pecans, cherries, pineapple, and raisins, using the remaining ½ cup flour. Add to the creamed mixture. Beat the egg whites until very stiff. Carefully fold into the cake batter. Spoon into prepared pans and bake for 1½ hours at 300 degrees; then increase oven temperature to 350 degrees and bake 7 minutes longer. Turn off the oven and let cakes stay in the oven for 7 more minutes. Cool in pans on racks.

When cool, remove cakes from pans, wrap each in foil, and store in a cool place. Makes 3 fruit cakes.

FRUIT SHORTCAKE
Vern

My mother-in-law taught me how to make these shortcakes. I'd like to have a penny for every one I have made.

Milk (as needed)
1 egg, well-beaten
2 cups flour
4 tsp. baking powder

1 tsp. salt
2 tbsp. sugar
⅓ cup butter or shortening

Heat oven to 400 degrees. Lightly grease a baking sheet. In a mixing cup or bowl, add enough milk to the beaten egg to make 1 cup. Set aside.

In a large bowl, sift together flour, baking powder, and salt. Add sugar and stir to mix well. Cut ⅓ cup butter or shortening into flour mixture until it becomes like cornmeal. Add milk and egg mixture all at once and barely blend. Do not handle too much.

Turn out onto a floured board and knead 4 or 5 times. Pat out to ½-inch thickness, and cut with a biscuit or cookie cutter. Place apart on a greased baking sheet, and bake at 400 degrees until brown, about 12 minutes. Split while still hot. Makes 8 to 10 cakes, using a three-inch cutter. Using a smaller size cutter yields about 1½ dozen.

Note: Butter the shortcakes and serve covered with sweetened fruit. They're good with strawberries or fresh peaches. Whipped cream makes this a party dish.

FLUFFY FROSTING
Vern

1 tbsp. flour
½ cup milk
½ cup vegetable
shortening
½ cup granulated sugar

¼ tsp. salt
1 tsp. vanilla
1 cup confectioners' sugar
½ cup cocoa (optional)

In a saucepan over low heat, blend flour and milk, cooking and stirring until very thick. Remove from heat and cool. In the large bowl of an electric mixer, combine shortening, granulated sugar, salt, and vanilla. Add flour-milk mixture. Beat at high speed until no sugar grains remain, then add confectioners' sugar, mixing well. For chocolate frosting, add cocoa.

Makes enough to frost a 9 x 13 x 2-inch cake, or two 9-inch layer cakes.

Note: To make any confectioners' sugar frosting creamy, add 1 tablespoon flour. This recipe is an old stand-by that always turns out creamy and stays moist and soft.

CREAMY VANILLA PUDDING FROSTING
Vern

Use this frosting on a light cake, white or yellow.

1 pkg. (4-serving size)
instant vanilla pudding
mix
¼ cup confectioners' sugar

1 cup cold milk
1 carton (8 oz.) frozen
whipped topping,
thawed

In an electric mixer bowl, combine dry pudding mix, sugar, and milk. Beat slowly until well blended, about 1 minute. Fold in whipped topping. Refrigerate.

FESTIVE FILLING
Vern

Spread this filling between the layers of a white or yellow three-layer cake.

1½ cups commercial
eggnog
1 pkg. (3 oz.) lemon-
flavored gelatin

1 pt. ice cream, any flavor
½ cup mincemeat

In a medium-size saucepan, heat eggnog until hot but not boiling. Remove from heat and dissolve lemon gelatin in hot eggnog. Blend in slightly softened ice cream. Add mincemeat, mixing well. Chill. Spread filling between cake layers and frost with whipped cream.

Desserts and Candies

MOLASSES PUDDING
Elizabeth

1 egg
1 tbsp. sugar
6 tbsp. lard (shortening),
  melted
½ cup molasses
1 cup flour

Pinch salt
½ tsp. baking soda
½ tsp. cinnamon
¼ tsp. ginger
½ cup buttermilk

Beat the egg in a medium-size mixing bowl. Beat in sugar and melted shortening. Fold in molasses. In a small bowl, sift together flour, salt, baking soda, cinnamon, and ginger. Add flour mixture to molasses mixture. Stir in buttermilk and mix well.

Heat oven to 350 degrees. Pour into a small, flat vessel (an 8 x 8-inch pan) and bake for about 35 minutes. When toothpick inserted in center comes out clean, the cake is done. Serve hot with lemon sauce or milk.

PEACH LEATHER SWEETMEATS
Elizabeth

Children will love to make this recipe! These are much like today's fruit roll-ups. This recipe is included for its historical significance as well.

2 tbsp. butter (for
  greasing)

1 lb. peaches
¼ lb. sugar

Grease platters or a board well with butter. Small peaches may be used, but they must be unspecked. Wash, peel, cut in half, and remove stones from peaches. Combine fruit and sugar in a saucepan, without water, and place over the fire to stew. Bring to a boil and simmer for about 10 minutes.

Cook until fruit is soft, stirring and mashing as mixture simmers. When peaches reach a consistency at which they can be spread out in a thin sheet on the prepared platters or board, do so. Set the "leather" in the sun to dry. Protect the fruit from flies with cheese-cloth netting.

When dry, the leather can be rolled up or divided into smaller pieces. Sprinkle it lightly with sugar before rolling, then dip in sugar. Wrap in wax paper and then in cheesecloth. The sweetmeat will keep indefinitely. Makes 1 large or 3 to 4 smaller roll-ups.

JELLY FRITTERS
Elizabeth

2 eggs
1 cup milk
2 cups whole wheat flour
1 tsp. salt

1 tbsp. lard (shortening)
Favorite jelly or powdered
   sugar (optional)

In a medium-size mixing bowl, make a batter of eggs, milk, wheat flour, and salt. Beat until light. Put lard (shortening) or beef fat in a skillet, and heat until boiling.

Add batter by large spoonfuls, not too close together. When one side is delicate brown, turn the fritter and fry until light brown. Serve with your favorite jelly or powdered sugar. Yields 20 large fritters.

PLUM PUDDING
Elizabeth Jane

This family recipe is one my husband loved. You'll need two clean, one-pound coffee cans for cooking the pudding.

2 cups raisins
2 cups currants
1 cup flour
1 tsp. soda
¾ cup sour milk
2 eggs

¾ cup sugar
¼ cup molasses
1 cup chopped suet (¼ lb.)
1 cup bread crumbs
1 tsp. allspice
1 tsp. salt

Dredge raisins and currants with a little of the flour; set aside. In a large mixing bowl, dissolve soda in sour milk. In another bowl, beat eggs; then add sugar and molasses, mixing well. Add egg mixture to milk mixture. Stir in remaining flour, suet, bread crumbs, allspice, salt, floured raisins, and currants. Use more flour if needed to stiffen the batter. Mix well.

Heat a large kettle of water to boiling. Grease two 1-pound coffee cans and pour in pudding mixture, filling each half full. Lightly cover cans with foil. Place the cans in the large kettle of boiling water so that the water comes up almost to the top of the cans. Cover and steam for about 3 hours.

Remove both puddings from cans. Serve one pudding and save the other to be reheated and enjoyed later. (Wrap in foil and refrigerate.) Serve Plum Pudding hot with a dessert sauce, ice cream, or whipped cream. Yields 8 servings per can.

BREAD PUDDING
Jessie

4 slices stale bread, cut up
6 tbsp. brown sugar
2 tbsp. butter, melted
3 cups milk, scalded and
  cooled

3 eggs
¼ tsp. salt
1 tbsp. vanilla
½ cup raisins

Grease an 8 x 8-inch baking dish. In a mixing bowl, combine cut-up bread, sugar, butter, and milk. Beat eggs and add to bread mixture; mix well. Stir in salt, vanilla, and raisins.

Heat oven to 350 degrees. Pour pudding mixture into prepared baking dish and bake, uncovered, until done, about 45 minutes. Yields 6 generous servings.

BLUEBERRY BUCKLE
Jessie

Served with cream or half-and-half, this recipe is a dessert; but cut in squares, it's great with coffee as a coffeecake!

2 cups fresh blueberries	2 tsp. baking powder
¼ cup butter	½ tsp. salt (optional)
½ cup sugar	2 cups flour
1 egg	¾ cup milk

TOPPING:

¼ cup butter	½ cup flour
½ cup sugar	1 tsp. cinnamon

Wash blueberries, drain well, and set aside. Grease a 6½ x 10½ x 2-inch baking dish or pan and set aside. Heat oven to 375 degrees.

In a medium-size bowl, cream butter and sugar together. Add egg and mix well. In a small bowl, stir baking powder and salt into flour, then sift into creamed mixture. Stir, then gradually add milk, mixing well. Add fresh blueberries last, stirring gently to blend. Pour into prepared baking dish.

For the topping, melt butter in small saucepan. Remove from heat, then add sugar, flour, and cinnamon. Stir well until mixture is crumbly. Cover the blueberry buckle with topping. Bake at 375 degrees for 35 to 45 minutes. Serve warm, with cream if desired. Yields 8 servings.

RHUBARB CRISP
Jessie

4 cups pie plant (rhubarb), washed and cut in 1-inch pieces	3 tbsp. flour
	1 cup sugar
	2 tbsp. butter, melted

TOPPING:

1 cup flour
1 tsp. baking powder
1 cup sugar

½ tsp. salt
1 egg, beaten

Grease a 9 x 13 x 2-inch pan. Heat oven to 350 degrees. In a medium-size bowl, combine flour, sugar, and melted butter and mix in cut-up rhubarb. Pour into prepared pan.

For the topping, combine flour, baking powder, sugar, and salt in a small bowl. Stir in beaten egg, and sprinkle mixture on top of batter. Bake for 40 minutes. Yields 12 servings.

Note: Other fruits in season may be substituted for rhubarb.

STOVETOP RICE PUDDING
Vern

This pudding is ready to serve in less than an hour.

1 cup plus 1 tbsp. water
½ cup rice
1 qt. milk
½ cup sugar

1½ tsp. vanilla
1 tbsp. cornstarch
1 egg yolk, beaten
1 tsp. butter

In a large saucepan, heat 1 cup water to boiling. Stir in rice, bring to boil, and cook, uncovered, for 10 minutes, until water is absorbed. Stir in milk and return to a boil. Cook, uncovered, for 30 minutes, stirring often to prevent sticking. Stir in sugar and vanilla.

In a small bowl or cup, dissolve cornstarch in 1 tablespoon of water and stir into hot pudding. Cook for another 10 minutes. Add 4 tablespoons of the hot pudding to the egg yolk, stir well, and add to the main mixture. Cook for about 1 minute longer. Stir in butter. Yields 6 to 8 servings.

NO-BAKE CRACKER PUDDING
Vern

This pudding tastes best after being refrigerated.

2 pkg. (3 oz. each) instant
  coconut cream pudding
1 lb. whole graham
  crackers
1 carton (8 oz.) frozen
  whipped topping,
  thawed

2 squares unsweetened
  chocolate
1 tbsp. corn syrup
3 tbsp. margarine
1 tsp. vanilla
3 tbsp. milk
1½ cups powdered sugar

Butter a 9 x 13 x 2-inch pan or baking dish. Prepare pudding according to package directions. Place a layer of whole graham crackers on the bottom of prepared pan. Fold whipped topping into prepared pudding. Spread half the pudding over the layer of crackers. Add another layer of crackers, and top with remaining pudding. Finish with remaining crackers.

In a saucepan over low heat, melt chocolate with corn syrup and margarine, stirring constantly. Remove from heat and add vanilla and milk, mixing well. Beat in powdered sugar. Spread mixture over top layer of crackers. Refrigerate uncovered. Keeps in the refrigerator for two days. Yields 15 servings.

SALTED CRACKER PUDDING
Vern

This is a rich dessert, so cut it in small portions.

12 salted crackers
12 graham crackers
¼ cup sugar
¼ cup margarine, melted
2 pkg. (3 oz. each) instant
  vanilla pudding
2 cups milk

1 qt. butter brickle ice
  cream, softened
1 carton (8 oz.) frozen
  whipped topping,
  thawed
2 Heath candy bars (1.4
  oz. each)

Using a 9 x 13 x 2-inch baking dish or pan, crush crackers, stir in sugar and margarine, and press mixture to form a crust. Do not bake.

Prepare instant vanilla pudding, using 2 cups of milk instead of the 4 directed on the packages. Beat ice cream into prepared pudding and pour mixture onto the crust. Refrigerate. When dessert congeals, spread on whipped topping. Using a nut chopper, blender, or food processor, crush the candy bars. Garnish with chopped candy. Store in refrigerator before serving, and refrigerate any leftovers. Yields 15 servings.

APRICOT OR PINEAPPLE TARTS
Vern

Pie crust for tarts	¼ tsp. vanilla
1 pkg. (3 oz.) cream cheese	1 cup sour cream
¼ cup sugar	1 cup canned apricots or pineapple, drained and cut-up
¼ tsp. salt	

Use any good pie crust recipe. (See index for Vern's or Jessie's) Line 8 tart pans with crusts. Prick each with a fork to keep tarts from shrinking. Bake the tart shells at 350 degrees for about 10 minutes or until brown. Cool.

In a mixing bowl, cream the cream cheese and sugar; then add salt and vanilla. Blend in sour cream and sliced apricots or pineapple, using as much fruit as needed to fill shells. Fill shells with fruit mixture. Refrigerate until serving. Yields 8 tarts.

APPLE DUMPLINGS
Vern

SYRUP:

2 cups sugar	¼ cup butter
¼ tsp. cinnamon	¼ tsp. nutmeg
2 cups water	

DUMPLINGS:

2 cups flour
2 tsp. baking powder
1 tsp. salt

¾ cup shortening
½ cup milk

FILLING:

¼ cup sugar
1 tsp. cinnamon

¼ tsp. nutmeg
6 apples, peeled and cored

Combine the syrup ingredients in a saucepan and boil for 5 minutes to make syrup. Set aside.

In a mixing bowl, combine flour, baking powder, and salt. Cut the shortening into the dry ingredients as if making pie dough. Stir in milk to form a dough. On a floured board, roll dough as thin as pie pastry, then cut into six 6-inch squares. Heat oven to 375 degrees.

In a small bowl, combine sugar, cinnamon, and nutmeg. Cut apples fine and place equal amounts on half of each dough square. Sprinkle ½ to ¾ teaspoon of sugar mixture on the apples on each square, as desired. Fold other half of each dough square over the apples and crimp edges, or gather dough completely around filling, pinching at the top.

Place all six dumplings in a 9 x 13 x 2-inch pan or on a jelly-roll baking pan and pour hot syrup over dumplings. Bake at 375 degrees for 30 minutes, basting occasionally with syrup. The syrup will cook down and thicken.

When serving, place a dumpling in an attractive dish and spoon some of the remaining syrup on top. Yields 6 servings.

PEACHY PAN DANDIES
Vern

Once, when apples were not available for dumplings and peaches were, I created this recipe. Any fresh fruit would be good!

1 recipe Apple Dumplings
dough and syrup (recipe
above)

6 large fresh peaches
½ cup candied cherries
Sugar (to sweeten)

Prepare the syrup and dough as if making apple dumplings (recipe above). Wash and peel the peaches, cut them in half, and carefully remove the pits. Fill each half with candied cherries. Put the two halves of each peach together again, and place each one on a square of dough. Sprinkle liberally with sugar. Or, roll each in sugar before placing on dough. Gather dough around each peach.

Heat oven to 350 degrees. Arrange dandies in a 9 x 13 x 2-inch baking pan, and cover with hot syrup. Bake for 35 minutes. Yields 6 servings.

BUSTER BROWN ICE CREAM DESSERT
Vern

1 cup butter or margarine,
melted
1 lb. Oreo cookies,
crushed
½ gallon vanilla ice cream,
softened
1 jar (11.5 oz.) commercial
chocolate topping

1½ cups Spanish peanuts
2 cups powdered sugar
1½ cups evaporated milk
⅔ cup chocolate chips
1 tsp. vanilla

Combine half of the melted butter or margarine with the crushed cookies, then press into a 9 x 13 x 2-inch baking dish. Spread on softened ice cream to make the second layer. Pour on chocolate topping. Freeze until crust and ice cream are firm. Sprinkle Spanish peanuts on top.

In a saucepan, combine powdered sugar, evaporated milk, remaining butter or margarine, and chocolate chips; bring to a boil and cook for 8 minutes. Remove from heat and add vanilla. Cool. Pour on top of dessert. Freeze for at least 24 hours before serving. Yields 18 to 20 servings.

BLUEBERRY OR FRUIT
PIE FILLING DESSERT
Vern

16 graham crackers,
crushed fine
1 cup sugar, divided
½ cup butter or
margarine, softened
1 pkg. (8 oz.) cream
cheese, softened

2 eggs, beaten
1 can (21 oz.) pie filling
(any flavor)
Ice cream (optional)

In a mixing bowl, combine cracker crumbs, ½ cup sugar, and butter or margarine. Mix well and press into a 9 x 13 x 2-inch baking dish to form a crust. Do not bake. Heat oven to 350 degrees.

In a small bowl, mix cream cheese, ½ cup sugar, and eggs together until light and fluffy. Spread over crumb crust, and bake at 350 degrees for 20 minutes. Cool. Spread prepared pie filling (blueberry, strawberry, and cherry are favorites) over top of pie. Refrigerate until serving. Top with ice cream, if desired. Yields 12 servings.

BRANDIED BOMBE
Vern

When you want to make a big impression, bring this one out on your most elegant plate!

¼ cup brandy
1 cup drained, pitted,
dark, sweet cherries
1 qt. vanilla ice cream
1 qt. chocolate ice cream

1 cup whipping cream
1 drop red food coloring
Chocolate curls (for
garnish)

In a small bowl, pour brandy over cherries; cover and let stand 6 hours. In a 9-inch bowl (4½ inches deep), soften the vanilla ice cream and mold it to form a shell about 2 inches thick. Freeze until firm.

Soften chocolate ice cream and stir in the brandy and cherries. Spoon chocolate ice cream-cherries mixture into the vanilla ice cream shell. Cover and freeze until firm.

Unmold onto a serving plate and return Bombé to freezer. Whip the cream until thick. Add a drop of red food coloring to make it a pretty pink. Remove Bombé from freezer, spoon the whipped cream into a decorator bag, and form rosettes around the edges; or frost the Bombé with the whipped cream. Garnish with chocolate curls. Yields 10 to 12 servings.

Note: To make curls, use cold, preferably frozen, chocolate. With a vegetable parer, slowly peel off curls.

CHOCOLATE DELIGHT
Vern

½ cup margarine, melted
1 cup flour
½ cup chopped pecans
1 pkg. (8 oz.) cream
   cheese, softened
1 cup powdered sugar
1 8-oz. carton frozen
   whipped topping,
   thawed
1 pkg. (3 oz.) chocolate

instant pudding mix
1 pkg. (3 oz.) vanilla
   instant pudding mix
3 cups milk
1 16-oz. carton frozen
   whipped topping,
   thawed (optional)
Chopped nuts (optional)
Ice cream (optional)

Heat oven to 325 degrees. In a small bowl, combine melted margarine, flour, and ½ cup chopped pecans; mix well. Press mixture into a 9 x 13 x 2-inch baking dish. Bake at 325 degrees for 25 minutes. Cool.

Beat cream cheese with powdered sugar and fold in 8-oz. carton of the whipped topping. Spread on cooled crust. Beat instant pudding mixes with 3 cups of milk. Spread on top of cream cheese layer. For top layer, spread remainder of the whipped topping over the pudding layer and sprinkle with nuts. Refrigerate, uncovered, until serving. Or, omit top layer of whipped topping and chopped nuts and serve with ice cream. Makes 15 servings.

CHOCOLATE DATE DESSERT
Vern

15 cream-filled chocolate
  cookies (packaged),
  crushed
⅓ cup butter or
  margarine, melted
1 pkg. (8 oz.) pitted dates,
  cut up
¾ cup water

¼ tsp. salt
2 cups miniature
  marshmallows
½ cup chopped pecans
1 carton (8 oz.) frozen
  whipped topping,
  thawed
Pecan halves (to garnish)

Spread cookie crumbs in a 9 x 13 x 2-inch baking dish. Stir in melted butter and press mixture into dish to form a crust. In a saucepan, combine dates, water, and salt. Bring to a boil, reduce heat, and simmer for 3 minutes. Remove from heat, add marshmallows, and stir until dissolved. Cool to room temperature. Stir in chopped nuts.

Spread date mixture over crumbs in dish. Spread whipped topping over date layer, as desired. Garnish with pecan halves. Cover and chill overnight. Cut into squares to serve. Yields 12 to 16 servings.

GRAHAM CRACKER MERINGUE
Vern

Inexpensive and delightful, this dish is easy to prepare, but it is rich, so cut small servings.

3 egg whites, at room
  temperature
1 cup sugar
11 graham crackers,
  crushed

1 tsp. baking powder
½ cup chopped nuts
Ice cream

Heat oven to 350 degrees. Generously grease a 9-inch pie plate. In the large bowl of an electric mixer, beat egg whites until foamy. Slowly add sugar, continuing to beat until stiff peaks form. Fold in crushed crackers, baking powder, and chopped nuts. Spread meringue in pie plate. Bake at 350 degrees for 30 minutes. Cool. Cut in pie wedges and serve with ice cream. Yields 8 servings.

LEMON LAYERED DESSERT
Vern

For variety, other flavors of pudding mix are suggested as substitutes for lemon. However, in summertime, lemon is especially good.

1 cup flour
1 cup chopped pecans
1 stick margarine, melted
1 carton (8 oz.) frozen
 whipped topping,
 thawed
1 pkg. (8 oz.) cream
 cheese, softened

1 cup powdered sugar
2 pkg. (3 oz. each) instant
 lemon pudding mix
3 cups milk
Crushed pecans or Heath
 candy bars for garnish
 (optional)

Heat oven to 350 degrees. In a small bowl, combine flour, chopped pecans, and margarine; then press mixture into a 9 x 13 x 2-inch pan to form a crust. Bake for 15 minutes. Cool.

In a bowl, blend together 2 cups of whipped topping, cream cheese, and powdered sugar; spread on the baked crust. Prepare pudding mix according to package directions, using the 3 cups of milk. Spread over cream cheese layer. Frost with remaining 2 cups whipped topping. Sprinkle with crushed pecans or crushed Heath candy bars, if desired. Chill in refrigerator. To serve, cut into squares. Yields 12 to 16 servings.

MY SISTER JERRY'S
PINEAPPLE TORTE
Vern

1 can (20 oz.) crushed
pineapple, undrained
1¼ cups plus 2 tbsp.
sugar
2 tbsp. cornstarch
1½ cups flour

1 cup margarine, melted
6 egg whites
1 cup finely chopped nuts
1 carton (8 oz.) frozen
whipped topping,
thawed

In a saucepan, combine crushed pineapple with juice, 1¼ cups
sugar, and cornstarch. Bring to boil, and cook until thick. Cool. Set
aside.

In a bowl, combine flour, 2 tablespoons sugar, and margarine.
Press mixture into a 9 x 13 x 2-inch pan to form a crust. In the large
bowl of an electric mixer, beat egg whites until stiff. Fold in cooled
pineapple mixture and chopped nuts.

Heat oven to 350 degrees. Spread pineapple meringue over crust
and bake for 15 minutes. Reduce oven temperature to 300 degrees
and bake 15 minutes more. When cool, frost with whipped topping.
Yields 15 servings.

RHUBARB DESSERT
Vern

*Inexpensive to make and delicious, this dessert is like a pudding.
It's not as rich as the other desserts.*

4 to 5 cups fresh spring
rhubarb, cut in chunks
1 cup sugar
1 pkg. (3 oz.) strawberry
gelatin

½ cup butter, melted
1 cup water
Ice cream

Grease a 9 x 13 x 2-inch baking dish. Heat oven to 350 degrees. Spread fresh rhubarb in prepared pan to create a 2-inch layer. Sprinkle sugar and dry gelatin over top of rhubarb. Drizzle with melted butter and pour water over all. Bake at 350 degrees for 1 hour. Serve slightly warm with ice cream on top. Yields 12 to 15 servings.

BAKED CHRISTMAS CANDY
Vern

This recipe is baked in a pan and cut in squares like bars. It was a first-place winner in the Home for the Holidays Baking Fest sponsored by General Foods, Inc., WLLR/WMRZ Radio, and the Quad-City Times newspaper in Davenport, Iowa. Prizes were $100 and a Regal coffeemaker. I demonstrated this for home economics students at Bettendorf High School.

1 lb. flaked coconut
1 lb. pitted dates
6 oz. candied pineapple
1 pkg. (6 oz.) red candied cherries
1 pkg. (6 oz.) green candied cherries

1 cup chopped nuts (any kind)
1 can (14 oz.) sweetened condensed milk

Line a 9 x 13 x 2-inch pan with foil, lipping the foil over the edges. Butter both the pan and the foil. Heat oven to 250 degrees.

In a large mixing bowl, combine all ingredients and mix well. Press mixture into prepared pan and spread with your hands. Bake for 1 hour. Lift foil from pan, and remove candy from foil, peeling off the bottom foil. Place candy on a platter and when cool, and cut into 1½ inch squares. Yields approximately 30 pieces.

CORNFLAKES CANDY
Vern

9 cups cornflakes
1½ cups granulated sugar
½ tsp. salt
¾ cup light corn syrup

2 tsp. vanilla
½ cup chunky peanut
butter
Chopped nuts (optional)

Measure cornflakes into a large, buttered bowl. Combine sugar, salt, and corn syrup in a large saucepan. Insert a candy thermometer and bring mixture to a boil. Reduce the heat to medium and, watching thermometer, cook to hard-ball stage (250 degrees). Do not overcook. Remove from heat and stir in vanilla, peanut butter, and chopped nuts, if desired. Mix well. Pour this mixture over the cornflakes. Using a wooden spoon, work quickly to blend ingredients. Drop mixture by spoonfuls in clusters on wax paper. Store in an airtight container. Yields about 40 clusters.

CINNAMON SYRUP
Vern

This syrup gives a completely different flavor to pancakes or ice cream.

1 cup sugar
1 tsp. cinnamon
1 tbsp. flour

½ cup butter
1 cup boiling water

In a medium-size saucepan, combine all ingredients; mix well. Over high heat, bring mixture to a boil, then reduce heat and cook over medium-high heat until thick. Cool slightly before serving. Yields about 1 cup.

Pies and Pie Crusts

JESSIE'S PIE CRUST

2 cups flour
1 tsp. salt
1 cup lard, chilled

Ice water (no more than ¼ cup)

Using a pastry blender, crumble the flour, salt, and lard together in a bowl until pieces are the size of small peas. Sprinkle ice cold water, one tablespoon at a time, over the mixture, gently lifting the dough with a fork until it forms a ball. Divide dough in half. Roll out one half of the dough on a floured board or pastry cloth. Repeat with second half of dough. Makes a double 9-inch pie crust, or two single pie crusts.

VERN'S ALWAYS TENDER PIE CRUST

3 cups flour
½ tsp. salt
1 cup shortening, chilled

1 egg, beaten
1 tsp. vinegar
Water (as needed)

Combine flour with salt, then cut in shortening until particles resemble small peas. Combine egg, vinegar, and enough water to make ½ cup in a glass measuring cup. Sprinkle the egg mixture gradually over flour mixture, and stir with a fork until dough forms a ball. Divide dough into thirds.

For each single crust, roll out one-third of the dough on a floured board or pastry cloth to fit a 9-inch pie plate. Flute edges after placing in pie tin or plate. Use with any pie recipe. Makes three single, 9-inch crusts.

GRAPE PIE
Lavina

Pastry for 2-crust, 9-inch
  pie
3 cups Concord grapes
1 cup sugar
3 tbsp. flour

1 tbsp. butter
Milk (for brushing on
  crust)
Sugar (to sprinkle on
  crust)

Slip skins from grapes. Place pulp in a medium-size saucepan. Set skins aside. Bring pulp to a boil and cook until seeds are loose. Remove from heat and press mixture through a sieve to remove the seeds. Discard seeds. Return pulp to saucepan; add skins. Combine 1 cup sugar with flour, then add to pulp and mix well. Bring to boiling over medium heat; cook and stir constantly until mixture thickens.

Heat oven to 400 degrees. Pour filling into a bottom crust. Dot with butter. Cover with top crust and cut slits into the top to allow steam to escape. Pie crust has a more attractive appearance if brushed with milk and sprinkled with sugar. Bake at 400 degrees for 40 minutes, or until top crust is nicely browned. Serves 6 to 8.

Note: This recipe uses Concord grapes, as it was prepared in earlier times. However, our recipe tester, Cindee Schnekloth of Eldridge, used a newer variety of grape, black seedless grapes, for her version. She just omitted the skinning and sieving procedures, and cooked the grapes with skins in a large saucepan.

CUSTARD PIE
Lavina

1 unbaked pie shell
1 cup sugar
5 eggs, well beaten
2 cups milk (1 percent
  works well)

1 tbsp. butter (or
  margarine)
2 tsp. vanilla
¼ tsp. salt
Nutmeg

In a mixing bowl, add sugar to eggs and beat well, until mixture is creamy. (Electric mixer works well.) Heat milk to scalding, but do not boil. Slowly add hot milk, stirring constantly, then add butter or margarine, vanilla, and salt. Beat until foamy.

Heat oven to 400 degrees. Pour filling into a 9-inch unbaked crust. Bake at 400 degrees for 10 minutes, then reduce heat to 300 degrees. Bake about 45 minutes, or until the custard sets. Sprinkle nutmeg on top for color and flavor. Serves 6 to 8.

VINEGAR PIE
Lavina

Housewives made this pie when fresh apples or lemons were scarce or as an alternative to raison pie.

2 tbsp. butter	**¼ tsp. salt**
½ cup sugar	**1 egg**
3 tbsp. flour	**2 tbsp. vinegar**
1 tsp. cinnamon	**1 cup water**
¼ tsp. allspice	**1 baked 8-inch pie shell**

Cream butter and sugar together in a large mixing bowl. Add flour, cinnamon, allspice, salt, egg, vinegar, and water; mix well. Pour mixture into the top part of a double boiler and cook over hot water until filling is smooth and thick, stirring constantly so it won't burn. Pour filling into an 8-inch baked and cooled pie shell. Serves 6 to 8.

Note: Pie may be eaten as is or may be topped with meringue and browned lightly in the oven. If making a 9-inch pie, double the ingredients.

PIE PLANT (RHUBARB) PIE
Jessie

This is my favorite pie!

1 egg
1¼ cups sugar
2 to 3 cups pie plant
(rhubarb), cut into
chunks

Pastry for double-crust, 9-
inch pie
3 tbsp. flour

In a mixing bowl, beat the egg and add the sugar; mix well. Stir in pie plant. Prepare pastry for a double-crust pie, letting filling stand while you make the crust.

Heat oven to 350 degrees. Line 9-inch pie pan with pastry. Pour filling into bottom crust, sprinkle with flour, and cover with a top crust. Cut slits to allow steam to escape. Bake at 350 degrees for 1 hour. Serves 6 to 8.

SODA CRACKER PIE
Jessie

This is one pie that doesn't use a pie shell!

3 egg whites
¾ tsp. vinegar
1 cup white sugar
¾ tsp. baking powder

1 cup white soda cracker
crumbs
½ cup chopped nuts
½ cup chopped dates

Heat oven to 350 degrees. Grease a 9-inch pie pan. In a large mixing bowl, beat the egg whites until stiff. Fold in vinegar, sugar, and baking powder. Fold in the soda cracker crumbs, nuts, and dates. Turn mixture into prepared pie pan. Bake at 350 degrees for 35 minutes. Allow pie to cool slightly before serving. Serve with whipped cream or ice cream. Serves 6 to 8.

DUTCH APPLE PIE
Jessie

1 9-inch pastry shell
1 cup sugar, divided
2 tbsp. flour
½ tsp. salt
6 to 8 apples, peeled,
    cored, and sliced

½ cup rich cream
1 tsp. cinnamon (optional)
Slices of cheese or ice
    cream

Heat oven to 350 degrees. Line a 9-inch pie tin with pastry. Sprinkle ½ cup sugar, flour, and salt on the pastry shell, then fill shell with sliced apples. Pour the cream over the sliced apples. Sprinkle with remaining ½ cup sugar and with cinnamon, if desired. Bake at 350 degrees for 45 minutes. Serve each piece of pie with a slice or wedge of cheese for color, or with ice cream. Serves 6 to 8.

ANY BERRY BERRY PIE
Vern

Use blackberries, loganberries, raspberries, or strawberries.

1 unbaked 9-inch pie shell
1 cup sugar
⅓ cup flour

4 cups fresh berries
2 tbsp. butter

Heat oven to 425 degrees. Roll out pie pastry to fit 9-inch pie plate. Place pastry in pie pan. In a mixing bowl, combine sugar, flour, and berries; turn into pie shell. Dot with butter. Cover with a top crust. Cut slits in top crust. Bake at 425 degrees for 45 minutes. If crust browns too quickly, reduce temperature to 350 degrees. Serves 6 to 8.

Note: If using large strawberries, you may want to cut them into smaller pieces.

CRANBERRY RAISIN PIE
Vern

I made this recipe up when I had just a few cranberries left over. It became my husband's favorite pie. For the pie crust, I use my own recipe, adding 2 tablespoons of brown sugar.

1 recipe Vern's Always Tender Pie Crust (for double-crust 9-inch pie)
1½ cups fresh cranberries
Water (to cover cranberries)
2 tbsp. flour
¼ cup water
¾ cup white raisins
1 cup plus 1 tbsp. white sugar
½ cup brown sugar
Milk (to brush pastry)
¼ cup finely chopped pecans

Heat oven to 350 degrees. In a saucepan, combine cranberries with barely enough water to cover and cook, stirring constantly until all skins pop. In a small measuring cup, moisten flour with ¼ cup water, stirring until mixture is smooth. Stir raisins, 1 cup white sugar, and brown sugar into boiling fruit; mix well. Slowly stir flour mixture into boiling fruit, and cook until thick.

Pour hot filling into unbaked bottom crust. Moisten the edges and cover with top crust, crimping the edges. Cut slits in top crust to allow steam to escape. Brush top crust lightly with milk and sprinkle with 1 tablespoon white sugar and pecans. Bake at 350 degrees for about 35 minutes, or until crust is brown and the filling bubbles out at the edges. Serves 6 to 8.

EASY STRAWBERRY PIE
Vern

1 9-inch pie shell, baked
and cooled
2 cups crushed, fresh
strawberries
2½ tbsp. cornstarch
⅔ cup sugar

3 drops red food coloring
2 cups fresh, hulled strawberries, whole or halves
Whipped cream dollops
(for garnish)
Ice cream (for topping)

Rinse and dry strawberries. In a saucepan, combine crushed strawberries with cornstarch and sugar; bring to a boil and cook until thick.
Stir in red food coloring. Cool. Put whole strawberries or strawberry
halves in a baked pie shell and pour on the cooled berry mixture.
Let set for 3 or 4 hours in the refrigerator. Top with whipped cream
or ice cream. Serves 6 to 8.

GLAZED PEACH PIE
Vern

This pie must be made with fresh, in-season, ripe peaches.

2½ cups peeled, pitted,
sliced fresh peaches
1 tbsp. lemon juice
¾ cup sugar
Water (as needed)
3 tbsp. cornstarch

⅛ tsp. salt
⅛ tsp. almond flavoring
2 tbsp. butter
1 baked 9-inch pie shell
Ice cream or whipped
cream

In a bowl, sprinkle peach slices with lemon juice. Add ¼ cup sugar,
and mix gently. Set aside for 1 hour. When time has elapsed, drain
peaches, reserving juice. Set peaches aside. Add enough water to
juice to make 1 cup.

In a saucepan, mix together the remaining ½ cup sugar and cornstarch. Add the juice-water mixture and cook rapidly until the liquid
is thick and clear. Remove from heat and stir in salt, almond flavoring,
and butter; mix well. Fold in reserved peaches. Turn filling into baked
pie shell and cool. Best served with ice cream or whipped cream.
Serves 6 to 8.

OPEN-FACED PEACH PIE
Vern

This is a family favorite!

1 9-inch unbaked pie shell
10 fresh or canned
  peaches
1 cup brown sugar

1 cup sour cream
4 tbsp. quick-cooking
  tapioca

Heat oven to 400 degrees. Peel and slice enough fresh peaches to fill an unbaked pie shell. Or, drain canned peach slices to fill the shell. Mix brown sugar, sour cream, and tapioca and spread over peaches. Bake at 400 degrees for 10 minutes. Reduce heat to 350 degrees and bake 45 minutes longer. The filling will set like a custard as it cools. Serve with ice cream or whipped cream. Serves 6 to 8.

MILE-HIGH MOCHA PIE
Vern

Easy and festive, this pie is a hit with coffee lovers.

1 cup strong, prepared
  coffee
½ lb. large or small
  marshmallows
1 tbsp. butter
1 container (8 oz.) frozen
  whipped topping,
  thawed

1 baked 9-inch pie shell
Chocolate sprinkles or
  shavings

To make the coffee, use 1 rounded tablespoon instant coffee in 1 cup hot water. Pour the coffee into a saucepan. Add marshmallows and butter. Cook over low heat until marshmallows are melted and mixture blends together. Remove from heat and cool until thick. Fold in whipped topping. Pour filling into baked pie shell and chill.

When pie is chilled, put chocolate sprinkles or shavings on top for accent. Serves 6 to 8.

SOUR CREAM RAISIN PIE
Vern

2 eggs, beaten
2 cups sour cream
¾ cup sugar
¼ tsp. salt
¼ tsp. ground cloves

1 tsp. cinnamon
½ tsp. nutmeg
2 cups raisins
1 unbaked 9-inch pie shell

Heat oven to 450 degrees. In a mixing bowl, combine beaten eggs with sour cream. Add sugar, salt, cloves, cinnamon, and nutmeg; mix well. Stir in raisins, mixing well. Pour filling into unbaked pie shell, and bake at 450 degrees for 10 minutes. Reduce temperature to 350 degrees, and bake 40 minutes longer. If preparing meringue, do not turn off oven. Top hot filling with meringue (recipe follows). Serves 6 to 8.

MERINGUE

3 egg whites, at room
  temperature
¼ tsp. cream of tartar

6 tbsp. sugar
½ tsp. vanilla

Oven temperature should be at 350 degrees. To make meringue, beat egg whites until foamy. Add cream of tartar and sugar, one tablespoon at a time, continuing to beat until whites are stiff and glossy. Fold in vanilla. Spread the meringue over the pie while the filling is still hot. Return to oven and bake at 350 degrees for about 10 minutes, watching carefully so that the meringue turns to a golden brown. Cool before serving. Covers 1 pie.

Cookies

SOFT MOLASSES COOKIES
Lavina

8 cups flour
1 tsp. baking soda
1 tsp. baking powder
¼ tsp. salt
1 tbsp. ginger
1 tsp. cinnamon

3 cups molasses
1 cup lard, melted
½ cup butter, melted
10 tbsp. boiling water
Sugar (for sprinkling)

In a large mixing bowl, sift 4 cups of flour with the baking soda, baking powder, salt, ginger, and cinnamon. In another bowl, combine molasses, melted lard, melted butter and boiling water; mix well. Add to the flour mixture; mix well. Stir in the remaining flour. Chill in refrigerator for 1 hour.

Heat oven to 375 degrees. Roll out dough on a lightly floured board to ¼-inch thickness. Cut with a cookie cutter and sprinkle with sugar. Bake on greased cookie sheets at 375 degrees for 8 minutes. Makes a large batch of cookies—more than 8 dozen if a 2½-inch fluted cookie cutter is used. Cookies freeze well.

SUGAR COOKIES
Lavina

1 cup margarine or
   shortening
3 cups flour
3 eggs
1 tsp. vanilla

1¼ cups white sugar
1 tsp. baking powder
½ tsp. nutmeg
¼ tsp. salt

Heat oven to 350 degrees. Grease cookie sheets. Slice margarine and cut it into the flour. In a small bowl or cup, beat the eggs together slightly with a fork and add the vanilla. In a large bowl, combine the flour mixture, sugar, baking powder, nutmeg, and salt. Add the eggs and vanilla mixture. Mix well and drop by teaspoonful onto a greased cookie sheet. Bake at 350 degrees for 12 to 15 minutes. Makes 3 dozen.

APRISCOTCH BARS
Vern

This is a popular recipe; it has been tested many times and was a winner in a cookie contest.

FILLING:

1 cup apricot pulp, from 1
  can (20 oz.) apricots
½ cup sugar
1 tbsp. flour

1 tbsp. lemon juice
2 tbsp. orange juice
2 tsp. butter

BARS:

3 cups flour
2 tsp. cream of tartar
1 tsp. baking soda
1 tsp. salt
1½ cups brown sugar

¾ cup vegetable
  shortening
2 eggs
Confectioners' sugar

Prepare apricot pulp. Drain canned apricots and purée fruit in a blender or put through sieve, mashing soft skins. In a saucepan, combine 1 cup apricot pulp, sugar, flour, lemon juice, orange juice, and butter. Bring to boil, reduce heat, and cook over low heat until well blended, stirring constantly for about 5 to 8 minutes. Set aside.

Grease a 9 x 13 x 2-inch pan. Heat oven to 350 degrees. In a mixing bowl, sift together flour, cream of tartar, baking soda, and salt. In another bowl, cream well the brown sugar and shortening. Add the eggs and mix well. Blend the flour mixture gradually into the creamed mixture. Dough will be crumbly. Press half of the dough in the prepared pan and spoon on the filling, spreading it evenly to the edges of the pan. Sprinkle remaining dough on top. It will spread in baking. Bake at 350 degrees for 25 to 30 minutes, or until brown. Cool slightly. Cut in bars and roll in confectioners' sugar. Makes about 3 dozen small bars.

Note: Apriscotch Bars also may be cut in squares and served with whipped cream or ice cream as a dessert.

CRANBERRY APRISCOTCH BARS
Vern

This recipe was a finalist in the 1988 Home for the Holidays Baking Fest sponsored by General Foods, Inc., WLLR/WMRZ Radio, and Quad-City Times in Davenport, Iowa.

FILLING:

1 cup apricot pulp, from drained canned apricots
½ cup sugar
1 tbsp. flour
1 tbsp. lemon juice

2 tbsp. orange juice
2 tsp. butter
½ cup cooked cranberry sauce

BARS:

3 cups flour
2 tsp. cream of tartar
1 tsp. baking soda
1 tsp. salt

1½ cups brown sugar
¾ cup butter
2 eggs
1 cup flaked coconut

To make filling, combine apricot pulp, sugar, flour, lemon juice, orange juice, butter, and cranberry sauce in a saucepan; mix well. Bring to a boil, reduce heat, and cook over low heat for 5 to 8 minutes, stirring constantly because mixture burns easily. Set aside.

Grease a 9 x 13 x 2-inch baking pan. Heat oven to 350 degrees. Sift dry ingredients together in a mixing bowl. In another bowl, cream brown sugar and butter; then add eggs and beat well. Add coconut. Stir in the dry ingredients with a spoon. Dough will be crumbly. Press half of the crumbly dough into the greased baking pan. Spoon on the filling, spreading it to the edges. Sprinkle the remaining dough over the filling. Dough will spread in baking. Bake at 350 degrees for 25 to 30 minutes. Cool slightly. Cut in bars and roll in confectioners' sugar. Makes about 3 dozen small bars.

DOUBLE CHOCOLATE CARAMEL BARS
Vern

This recipe was also selected as a finalist in the 1988 Home for the Holidays Baking Fest.

1 pkg. (18.25 oz.) cake
   mix (chocolate or white)
½ cup chopped walnuts
1 cup evaporated milk

¼ cup butter, melted
¾ cup chocolate chips
½ cup commercial caramel
   ice cream topping

Heat oven to 350 degrees. Grease a 9 x 13 x 2-inch baking pan. In a large mixing bowl, combine dry cake mix, chopped walnuts, evaporated milk, and melted butter. Spread half of the mixture into the prepared baking pan. Bake at 350 degrees for 10 minutes.

Remove from oven and sprinkle on chocolate chips. Pour caramel ice cream topping over top. Spread remaining batter over the caramel. Return to oven and bake at 350 degrees for 20 to 25 minutes. Cut into bars while warm. Makes about 3 dozen bars.

NO-BAKE COOKIE BARS
Vern

Graham crackers
1 cup brown sugar
½ cup plus 2 to 3 tbsp.
   milk
½ cup plus 1 tbsp. butter
1 cup graham cracker
   crumbs

1 tsp. vanilla
½ cup chopped nuts
½ cup confectioners' sugar
1 tbsp. flour

Butter a 9 x 13 x 2-inch pan or dish, and line it with whole graham crackers. In a saucepan, combine the brown sugar, ½ cup milk, and ½ cup butter; bring to a boil and cook for 2 minutes, stirring constantly. Remove from the heat and add graham cracker crumbs and vanilla. Pour over the layer of crackers. Add nuts, pressing them down. Cover with another layer of whole graham crackers. In a mixing bowl, beat the confectioners' sugar, flour, and 1 tablespoon butter, adding enough milk to achieve a spreading consistency. Beat together until smooth, then spread on top of graham crackers. Let set for 1 hour before cutting into bars. Makes about 3 dozen bars.

CANDY COOKIES
Vern

1½ cups finely chopped
  Heath candy bars
1½ cups flour
2 tsp. baking soda
½ tsp. salt

½ cup butter or margarine
¾ cup brown sugar
1 egg
1 tsp. vanilla
¼ cup chopped pecans

Grease baking sheets. Finely chop Heath candy bars to measure 1½ cups; set aside. Heat oven to 350 degrees.

In a small bowl, sift together the flour, baking soda, and salt. In another bowl, cream the butter, brown sugar, egg, and vanilla. Stir the dry ingredients into the creamed mixture. Blend in the chopped candy bars and nuts. Drop dough by tablespoonful onto greased baking sheets. Bake at 350 degrees for 12 to 15 minutes. Remove from pans at once. Makes 3 dozen cookies.

CHOCOLATE MALTED MILK SQUARES
Vern

1 cup plus 2 tbsp. flour
⅓ cup shortening
½ cup brown sugar
2 eggs
⅔ cup granulated sugar
½ cup powdered chocolate
  malted milk

½ tsp. baking powder
¼ tsp. salt
1 cup coconut
1 cup chopped nuts

Heat oven to 350 degrees. In a mixing bowl, combine 1 cup flour, shortening, and brown sugar; mix well and press into a 8 x 12-inch baking dish or pan. Bake at 350 degrees for 10 minutes.

In a mixing bowl, beat the eggs with the granulated sugar. Sift together in a small bowl the 2 tablespoons flour, powdered chocolate malted milk, baking powder, and salt. Stir into egg-sugar mixture. Spread over crust. Sprinkle coconut and nuts on top. Bake at 350 degrees for 20 to 25 minutes. Cut into 1½ inch squares. Makes 48 squares.

FROSTED DROP COOKIES
Vern

This is a delicious, soft drop cookie.

½ cup butter or margarine	1 tsp. baking soda
1½ cups brown sugar	½ tsp. baking powder
1 tsp. vanilla	½ tsp. salt
2 eggs	1 cup sour cream
2½ cups flour	½ cup chopped nuts

FROSTING:

6 tbsp. butter	Pecan or walnut halves
1 tsp. vanilla	(optional)
2 cups confectioners'	Red or green maraschino
sugar	cherries (optional)
Hot water	

Heat oven to 350 degrees. Grease cookie sheets. In a mixing bowl, cream butter, brown sugar, and vanilla. Beat in eggs, and continue beating until mixture is light and fluffy.

In another bowl, sift together the flour, baking soda, baking powder, and salt. Add dry ingredients to the creamed mixture alternately with the sour cream. Stir in the nuts. Drop dough by teaspoonfuls about 2 inches apart on a greased cookie sheet. Bake at 350 degrees for 10 to 12 minutes, until browned. Cool.

To make frosting, heat butter in a saucepan and stir until golden brown. Remove from heat and beat in confectioners' sugar and vanilla. Add enough hot water to create a smooth consistency for spreading. Frost each cookie and garnish with half a nut or red or green maraschino cherries (optional). Makes about 4½ dozen cookies.

GUM DROP BARS
Vern

1½ cups flour
1 tsp. baking powder
½ tsp. salt
1 tsp. cinnamon
⅓ cup soft shortening
1 cup brown sugar
1 egg

2 tsp. vanilla
¼ cup evaporated milk
1 cup small soft, gum
  drops (any kind except
  licorice)
½ cup chopped nuts
Confectioners' sugar

Heat oven to 350 degrees. Grease a 9 x 9-inch baking dish. In a small bowl, sift together the flour, baking powder, salt, and cinnamon; set aside. In a large bowl, mix the shortening, brown sugar, egg, and vanilla with a wooden spoon. Stir in half the flour mixture and the evaporated milk; mix well. Stir in remaining flour mixture, gum drops, and nuts, blending well.

Spread dough in the prepared baking dish. Bake at 350 degrees for 30 minutes. Remove and place on a wire rack to cool. Cut in bars while still slightly warm; roll each bar in confectioners' sugar. Makes about 3 dozen bars.

NO-BAKE ORANGE BALLS
Vern

1 stick margarine,
softened
1 box (1 lb.) confectioners'
sugar
1 can (6 oz.) orange juice
concentrate, thawed

1 box (16 oz.) vanilla
wafers, crushed
2 cups chopped nuts or 2
cups flaked coconut

In a mixing bowl, blend together softened margarine, confectioners' sugar, and undiluted orange juice. Add the vanilla wafer crumbs, and mix well. Form into small balls, and roll each in nuts or coconut. For variety, roll in some of each! Makes about 3 dozen.

NO-SUGAR CHEESE COOKIES
Vern

This recipe tastes like a cracker and is excellent as an appetizer or for guests who can't eat sugar.

½ lb. sharp cheddar
cheese, shredded
½ cup margarine, softened
1 cup plus 2 tbsp. flour

¼ tsp. salt
Dash cayenne pepper
Pecan halves (optional)

In a bowl, blend shredded cheese into the softened margarine. Add flour, salt, and cayenne pepper; mix well and shape into two rolls. Wrap each roll in wax paper and refrigerate overnight.

Heat oven to 325 degrees. Cut dough into thin slices and garnish each slice with a pecan half if desired. Place on ungreased baking sheets and bake at 325 degrees for 10 to 13 minutes. Watch carefully because they will brown easily. Makes about 2 dozen cookies.

OLD TIME SUGAR COOKIES
Vern

1 cup margarine
1½ cups sugar
2 eggs
3 cups flour
½ tsp. salt

1 tsp. baking soda
2 tsp. cream of tartar
2 tsp. vanilla
Sugar (for dipping and
rolling)

Cream margarine and 1½ cups sugar in a mixing bowl. Beat in eggs until the mixture is very creamy. In a large bowl, combine flour, salt, soda, and cream of tartar, blending well. Stir flour mixture into creamed mixture, mixing well. Stir in vanilla. (I use my hands for a well-blended effect.) Chill dough in refrigerator for 1 hour.

Preheat oven to 350 degrees. Form dough into small balls. Dip and roll each ball in white sugar. Place on greased cookie sheets. Dip a fork in sugar so it won't stick and press down cookies. Bake at 350 degrees for 8 to 10 minutes, until light brown. Remove from pans to cool. Makes about 5 dozen cookies.

PINK COOKIES
Vern

2½ cups flour
2 tsp. baking powder
½ tsp. salt
1 cup shortening
⅔ cup white sugar

1 egg
1 tsp. vanilla
1 cup drained, ground
maraschino cherries
½ cup nuts

In a mixing bowl, sift the flour, baking powder, and salt. In another bowl, cream shortening and sugar. Beat in the egg and vanilla. Stir in cherries, flour mixture, and nuts, blending well. Chill dough in refrigerator for several hours.

Heat oven to 350 degrees. Drop dough by teaspoonful onto greased cookie sheets. Flatten dough with a glass dipped in sugar. Bake at 350 degrees for 8 to 10 minutes, watching carefully, until light brown. Yields about 4 dozen cookies.

ROLLED GINGER COOKIES
Vern

This is a great recipe for making gingerbread people.

1 cup sugar
1 cup sorghum or
  molasses
½ cup strong coffee
1 cup shortening

5 cups sifted flour
2 eggs, well-beaten
1 tbsp. baking soda
½ to 1 tbsp. ginger
½ tsp. salt

In a large saucepan, combine the sugar, sorghum or molasses, coffee,and shortening and boil for 5 minutes, stirring to mix well. Remove from the heat and cool slightly. Stir in 2 cups of the sifted flour, eggs, baking soda, ginger, and salt, blending well. Let cool, then add remaining flour. Chill thoroughly in refrigerator.

Heat oven to 375 degrees. Roll out dough on lightly floured board to ¼-inch thickness, then cut with a cookie cutter into desired shapes. Bake at 375 degrees for 6 to 8 minutes, so still soft to touch. Makes 4 to 5 dozen cookies.

TWINKLE TOP ORANGIES
Vern

This recipe was published in The Leader, *a weekly newspaper serving Scott County, Iowa. One day, the telephone rang. A woman called to tell me she sent a box of these cookies to her daughter in California. Her daughter later called long distance for the recipe.*

Juice of 1 orange
1 cup sugar, divided
2¼ cups flour
½ tsp. salt
1 tsp. baking soda
1 tsp. cream of tartar

¼ cup butter
¾ cup margarine
½ cup brown sugar
1 egg
1 tbsp. grated orange rind

Grease a large cookie sheet. Squeeze the juice from the orange into a cereal bowl and set aside. In a saucer, measure ½ cup of the white sugar and set aside for dipping. Heat oven to 350 degrees.

In a bowl, sift together the flour, salt, baking soda, and cream of tartar. In a large mixing bowl, cream butter, margarine, brown sugar, and remaining ½ cup white sugar with a big spoon until very creamy. Add egg and grated orange rind to creamed mixture; blend well. Stir in flour mixture. Form dough into small balls. Dip each ball in the orange juice, then roll it in sugar. Place on a greased cookie sheet. Bake at 350 degrees for 8 to 10 minutes. Remove from pans at once. Makes 3 dozen.

VERN'S OLD STAND-BYS

For a tea or coffee, I make these small. For grandchildren, I make them big and fat!

3 cups flour	1 egg
1 tsp. baking soda	3 tsp. vanilla
1 tsp. cream of tartar	1 cup quick-cooking oats
1 cup white sugar	1 cup Rice Crispies cereal
1 cup brown sugar	1 cup flaked coconut
1 cup margarine	1 pkg. (12 oz.) chocolate
1 cup vegetable oil	chips

In a bowl, sift together the flour, baking soda, and cream of tartar. In a large mixing bowl, cream the sugars, margarine, and oil. Add the egg and beat well. Stir in vanilla. Beat in with a spoon the flour mixture, oats, Rice Crispies cereal, coconut, and chocolate chips. Heat oven to 325 degrees.

Drop dough by spoonful in any size you like on greased cookie sheets. Bake at 325 degrees for about 12 minutes, or until browned. Makes about 5 dozen cookies.

The memory jug was a gift from a friend in Tipton Iowa, whose husband used it to carry water to the fields. It was covered with window putty, and keepsakes were arranged and pushed into the sides of the jug. Among other items, Vern displays her mother's and grandmother's wathch fobs, as well as a bracelet purchased in Nassau in 1965, her mother's thimble, cufflinks she gave to Rex, and a necklace her daughter Doris wore at her wedding. *Photo by Connie Heckert.*

Recommended Reading

American Cookery Manuscripts. c. 1759 (from the Collection of Chef Louis Szathmary II of Chicago, donated to the University of Iowa Libraries, Iowa City, Iowa).

Carpenter, Allan. *The Enchantment of America: Kentucky.* Illinois: Children's Press, 1967, 1979.

Dunne, E. F. *History of Illinois.* Chicago and New York: Lewis Publishing Company, 1933.

Gillette, F. L., and Hugo Ziemann. *The White House Cook Book.* Chicago: R.S. Peale & Company, 1890.

Guthrie, Margaret E. *The Best Midwest Restaurant Cooking.* Ames, Iowa: Iowa State University Press, 1989.

Hachten, Harva. *The Flavor of Wisconsin.* Madison, Wisconsin: The State Historical Society of Wisconsin, 1981.

Jones, Margaret. "The Changing Style in Cookbooks: It's Back to Basics with a Twist." *Publishers Weekly* (September 8, 1989): 15-18.

Morse, Sidney. *The New Household Discoveries.* New York, Ohio, Illinois, Oklahoma, California: The Success Company, 1908. (This book was passed down four generations to Connie Heckert.)

Neill, E. *The Everyday Cookbook: An Encyclopedia of Practical Recipes.* San Francisco: The Examiner Press, 1889. (This book was passed down through generations to Jessie Vernadine DeMoney Berry, and willed to her granddaughter.)

Pelton, Belulah Meier. *We Belong to the Land: Memories of a Mid-westerner.* Iowa State University Press.

The Best Yet Cook Book: An Every Day Guide for the Millions to Economical and Practical Cooking. Ohio: S.A. Milliken Company, 1907.

Smith, Elmer, ed. *Early Household Remedies.* Pennsylvania: Applied Arts Publishers, 1984.

Smith, Elmer, ed. *Household Tools and Tasks.* Pennsylvania: Applied Arts Publishers, 1984.

Sparkman. *American Cookery Manuscripts.* 82, c. 1850-1870 (from the Collection of Chef Louis Szathmary II of Chicago; donated to the University of Iowa Libraries, Iowa City, Iowa).

Townsend, Abigail Wellington. American Cookery Manuscripts. 58, c. 1800 (from the Collection of Chef Louis Szathmary II of Chicago; donated to the University of Iowa Libraries, Iowa City, Iowa).

Walker, Barbara Muhs. *The Little House Cookbook.* New York: Harper & Row, Inc., 1979.

Index